# River Reflections

*Outdoor Devotional Series*

# River Reflections

## Patty Mondore

*North Wind Publishing*
Belfast, Maine

North Wind Publishing
P.O. Box 8
Belfast, ME 04915
northwindpublishing.com

10 9 8 7 6 5 4 3 2 1

ISBN 978-0-9846946-3-1

Library of Congress Control Number: 2012943236

All photos by the author unless otherwise indicated.

Bookstores/Giftshops: Bulk ordering is available. Contact info@northwindpublishing.com.

# Dedication

*I am so thankful that God gave me a husband, a best friend, and a fellow River-lover (all rolled into one) to navigate through this life with, and to cruise on the River of Life together in the next. I love you, Bob! And, of course, there would be no* River Reflections *if it weren't for the One who created water, husbands, and the ability to love them all.*

# Publisher's Note

*Let the rivers clap their hands . . . .(Psalm 98:8)*

*River Reflections* by Patty Mondore spoke to me immediately when I first saw the manuscript. I have lived on or near water my entire life and can't imagine living anywhere else. The view above is the Passagassawakeag River in Belfast, Maine which empties into Penobsoct Bay. The Passy, as the locals call it, is right outside my office. I've seen bald eagles, hawks, cormorants, ducks, geese, loons, and seagulls hunting. On a hot day, birds will circle above the river taking advantage of the updrafts. The window behind my computer looks out at the river and I've been distracted more than once by a bird diving for food.

    *River Reflections* is a 90-day Devotional and Journal to help you with your bible study and meditations. Each day starts with a beautiful black and white river photo and bible verse. *River Cruise,* steers you toward portions of the bible you should read that day while *River Reflections* are the author's personal experiences living on the water and where she relates that experience to biblical teachings. *Waterlines* is an area for the reader to write down personal thoughts for the day, so this book becomes a keepsake journal. May God bless you and yours.

JANET ROBBINS, Publisher

# Introduction

*Devotions by the Water*

It isn't what I am leaving behind that drives me out of the office on a beautiful summer day by 5:01 P.M. It's where I am going. I just can't wait to be able to spend time by the water. I suppose my love of the water is partly because I grew up around it. Some of the earliest baby pictures I've seen of myself show me standing either by, or in the lake. I spent my life by the water and have often told people I have river water running through my veins instead of blood. I would rather be at the River than anywhere else in the world. Yet, I know my captivation with the water comes from more than just upbringing and familiarity. The special love I have for this wondrous creation is, I believe, a natural byproduct of my love for its Creator. Being by the water makes me feel closer to the God who made it. Oh, but it isn't just me! Just look at all the Scriptures that speak of the water. Why, Jesus, himself, spent a good deal of time by the water. We often find him using it in his parables and illustrations. Water even played a major role in several of the miracles he did. That is just one more reason why spending time by the water can deepen your faith.

Still not convinced? Then come and join me on a brief journey to the shore. See if you, too, don't come away with a greater appreciation of the water and of the God who created it. I'll take you to some of my favorite spots on the River. I'll point out some of the lovely creatures that live by and in the water. We'll go on a few boat rides, and perhaps we'll even catch a fish or two along the way. There's always an adventure to be had by the water. My hope is that you'll not only enjoy your visit but that, in the process, you will find your love for the Creator deepening as you share these *River Reflections* with me.

PATTY MONDORE

# River Reflections

# 1. It Was Very Good

> ". . . and the gathered waters He called
> 'seas' and God saw that it was good."
> *(Gen. 1:10)*

## The River Cruise
*Read: Genesis 1:1–31*

## River Reflections:

It was 5:01 P.M. on Friday and I was out the door. It was a hot summer evening and the River beckoned. I edged my way through the rush hour traffic along with countless other hot and harried drivers making the evening commute. Most were likely headed home to escape into their air conditioning. I, however, was headed to the River. Two hours later, after a refreshing swim in the cool water I climbed up to one of my favorite spots on this lovely earth; the dock. The River had washed away all of the physical heat of the day and as I gazed into its gently lapping waters, I felt the stresses, problems and concerns of the day being slowly washed away as well. Almost involuntarily, I found words of praise and adoration welling up in my heart. "Lord, you certainly knew what you were doing when you created water," I exclaimed in a silent prayer as I had done so many times before.

Water was, of course, just one small part of God's glorious creation. Every creature he made, every star, every mountain, every blade of grass was perfectly designed with a beauty all its own. The more I learn about nature and its every intricate detail, the more I can understand why God saw that it was good. In fact, when he was completely done, the Bible tells us "God saw all that he had made, and it was *very* good". So come away with me for a while to the water's edge. Let me introduce you to some of the wonders I have discovered here at the River. But don't be surprised if you find yourself joining along with me in praise of the Master Designer who made it all so very good.

## Waterlines

## 2. Manitoanna

*"A river watering the garden flowed from Eden;
from there it was separated into four headwaters."*
*(Gen. 2:10)*

### River Cruise
Read Genesis 2:1–15

### River Reflections:
We refer to it, simply, as "The River." It is officially called the
St. Lawrence Seaway. Covering a distance of over 2,340 miles,
it is the world's longest inland waterway forming a natural
border between Canada and the United States. A small part
of that journey includes the 35 mile stretch of water referred
to as the Thousand Islands which contains over 1700 islands.
Geologists tell us that the islands were once part of a mountain range that was reduced by glaciers and rivers to the
islands we endearingly refer to as the River today. The Native
Americans had a different explanation. They called the area
"Manitoanna" which means "garden of the Great Spirit."
They believed that the Great Spirit created a garden paradise
along the shore of a river hoping to bring peace to warring
tribes. When they continued to fight, he came back to earth
in frustration to reclaim his gift. He bundled his paradise up

in a blanket but as he headed towards the heavens the blanket tore. Paradise crashed into the water and broke into hundreds of islands creating the wonder that exists today.

The Lord did, indeed, create a garden paradise for us. He even placed a river there in the garden to water it. Thankfully, when we messed up, he didn't just pack up and go home. Though, for a time, we could no longer enjoy paradise, God remained faithful. He allowed us to enjoy all the rest of his earthly creation including the River. It is hard to imagine its beauty cannot compare to the paradise that once was. But it is a very lovely reminder of what once was, and of what will one day be again when our Creator comes to fully restore his Manitoanna here on earth.

## Waterlines

# 3. Save the River

*The Lord God took the man and put him in the Garden of Eden to work it and take care of it. (Gen. 2:15).*

## River Cruise
*Read Psalm 8:1–9*

## River Reflections:

One of my favorite sweatshirts has a picture of a Great Blue Heron in flight with the caption "Save the River" below it. The *Save the River* Organization is a group of individuals who are dedicated to preserving the natural beauty, the environment and the wildlife of the St. Lawrence Seaway and surrounding area. Such an undertaking is no small feat considering the continually growing industries being built on the River, oil spills by freighters, and the ever-increasing amount of tourists visiting the area. One of their goals is to raise the funds needed to tackle these major projects. Just as important is the goal of greater public awareness. By selling their sweatshirts, and distributing their bumper stickers and newsletters, they hope that others will come to see the importance and personal responsibility of keeping the River clean and beautiful.

The concept of caring for our environment isn't new. It originated with the user's manual we were given from the very start. When God first created humankind he gave us the privilege and responsibility of taking care of the earth and all of its living creatures. When he placed the man and woman in his Garden he gave them the prime directive to care for the river along with all the rest of his creation. Clearly, we have lost our way, both in our care of the environment and in our care for each other. However, it is not too late to get back to our original assignment. It begins by returning to our Creator where we will be reunited with love, himself. As our love for him is rekindled so will our love for all of his creation. Filled with his love, we will find he can, indeed, use us to save the River, and so much more.

## Waterlines

# 4. The Snake

Photo by D. Gordon E. Robertson

*So the LORD God said to the serpent, "Because you have done this, Cursed are you above all the livestock and all the wild animals! You will crawl on your belly and you will eat dust all the days of your life."*
*(Gen. 3:14)*

## River Cruise
*Read Genesis 3:1–15*

## River Reflections:

My scream was probably heard over in Canada. "Don't worry. He's more scared of you than you are of him" the neighbor kids sputtered between gasps of hysteria. I had just stepped into the water for a swim when what looked like the biggest, blackest snake I had ever seen in my life slithered past me, out of the water and into the nearby rocks. I did what any normal, healthy, all-American woman would do. I screamed at the top of my lungs and ran for shore. The scare had been bad enough but to know I had provided such quality enter-tainment for the entire neighborhood made it even worse. "Yeah, right!" I thought to myself in response to their com-ment about it being more afraid of me. Somehow I couldn't imagine a snake thinking to itself, "Oh my, a skinny female human. I'm so afraid!" No, I was convinced that of the two of us, I was the one most traumatized by the ordeal. But somehow I felt justified in knowing I wasn't the first woman ever to have an upsetting encounter with a snake.

Eve was taken in at first when the serpent came and seduced her there in the Garden of Eden. But it wasn't until after she was deceived that the serpent ended up being "grounded" for his offense. Along with that punishment, God's curse upon Satan came with a promise: "And I will put enmity between you and the woman, and between your offspring and hers; he will crush your head, and you will strike his heel." (Gen. 3:15). One of Eve's future offspring, Jesus, would come and defeat this mortal enemy of mankind once and for all. Now that's exciting. But in the mean time, I'm still not going anywhere near those rocks.

## Waterlines

# 5. A Wall of Water

> The water flowed back and covered the chariots
> and horsemen—the entire army of Pharaoh
> that had followed the Israelites into the sea.
> Not one of them survived.
>
> (Ex. 14:28)

## River Cruise
Read Exodus 14:8–31

## River Reflections
I watched in awe as some very brave cameramen shot pictures of the ocean just as the hurricane hit shore. The TV screen showed boats tossed up onto the shore like bath toys, and buildings collapse like dominos as the wind-driven seas washed through. Despite all of our modern advances, we are as helpless to defend ourselves against the forces of nature as we were millennia ago. That is, unless the Creator himself should choose to intervene on our behalf. The people of Israel were finally headed to freedom. With Moses in the lead, this joyful multitude made their grand exodus from Egypt. Their joy was cut short, however, when they abruptly dead-ended at the seashore with their captors close behind in hot pursuit. Most commentators agree that the Red Sea in this spot was about 12 miles across and 28 yards deep. They were

stuck! But God was not about to lead his people this far only to abandon them. The waters divided before them forming two walls and a dry passage to walk through. No act of nature could have divided these waters and caused them to stand as a wall. In other words, it was a miracle.

There are, of course, skeptics who have tried to explain this all away. Some have theorized there was some kind of extraordinary ebb in the sea, or that a drought had lowered the water levels so they could have crossed on foot. But think about it. It would have been an even greater miracle for ankle deep waters to have wiped out an entire army including chariots and horsemen. No, he who created the mighty seas needed to but speak the word and the wall of water was in place just long enough for his people's safe passage.

## Waterlines

# 6. Don't Drink the Water

> *When they came to Marah, they could not drink its water because it was bitter.*
> *(Ex. 15:23)*

## River Cruise
*Read Exodus 15:1–23*

## River Reflections

The good news, I was told, was that our cottage on the River had running water. The bad news was that we couldn't drink it. That's because the water we would be using was pumped into the house directly from the River. While the St. Lawrence Seaway is considered one of the cleanest bodies of water in the State it is still not clean enough to drink. So at first we simply brought bottled water from home every time we came up. After several years of hauling water we decided to reevaluate the situation. My dad, the engineer, eventually came up with the perfect solution. He diverted one of the incoming water lines in the kitchen through a special filter. This fancy, high tech water purifier came with a guarantee that it removed 99.6% of all contaminants from the water. That's better than most city water providers can claim. And it's much better than hauling water.

11

In their travels through the desert the weary and very thirsty Israelites arrived at a place called Marah (which means "bitter"). It was so named because the water there was, quite literally, bitter. The people began to grumble not realizing they had a water purification system in their midst that could far surpass even the high tech model at our camp. God told Moses to throw a piece of wood into the bitter waters and when he did, they immediately became sweet so the people could freely drink (don't try this at home). Certainly, the Maker of water could make bitter water completely pure. Now just think! If we commit our bitter days to him, our Maker can use them to purify us. He can cause even the most difficult situations to work out for our eternal good. Hey, I'll drink to that!

## Waterlines

## 7. Elim

*Then they came to Elim, where there were twelve springs and seventy palm trees, and they camped there near the water.*
*(Ex. 15:27)*

### River Cruise
*Read Psalm 116:1–14*

### River Reflections

Our new neighbors all thought we were the Elim family. The day we moved into our new cottage on the River, my mom put a big sign out front that simply said, "Elim." Of course, we all knew why. When I was little we spent a few of our summer vacations at Elim Lodge, a family Bible camp on the Kawartha Lakes in Canada. It was there, that I heard my first loon cry at dusk, caught (actually *almost* caught) my first Muskie, learned to row a boat and was first left breathless by a sunset over the water. It helped that the other campers loved the water as much as we did. But it helped even more that most of them were there because they also loved its Creator. We spent many evenings singing songs of praise together with our fellow campers in the little chapel by the water. So it was no surprise when my mom pronounced our new camp, Elim!

There was another reason why the name Elim was so fitting for our camp. It goes back to the days when Moses and the Israelites were wandering in the wilderness. They had just passed through Marah where God had allowed them to experience its bitter waters. But from there he led them directly to Elim, a small piece of lush, waterfront property. There, he let them camp by the waters and relax for a while before continuing on their journey. Yes, God does allow us to go through difficulties and hardships at times. At other times, however, he brings us to a place of rest, a time of refreshment, an Elim. I thank God for our camp near the water, but I thank him even more for the Elim that can only be found in him.

## Waterlines

## 8. Strike the Rock

> *I will stand there before you by the rock at Horeb.*
> *Strike the rock, and water will come out*
> *of it for the people to drink.*
> *(Ex. 17:6)*

### River Cruise
Read Exodus 17:1–6, 1 Cor. 10:1–4

### River Reflections
It was one of the scariest days of my life. Bob and I planned
to meet at the marina in about 10 minutes. He would go by
boat and I would take the car. When I got to the marina I
went right to the dock. After 10 minutes, no Bob. After 20,
then 30 minutes had passed I was still waiting. Concern
moved to panic as I began envisioning the headline, "Bob
Mondore, Lost At Sea." Finally, bordering on hysteria, I spotted the familiar blue canvas top coming slowly around the
bend. The boat pulled into the dock with a weary looking
Bob at the helm. After ample hugs and kisses, he described
his adventure. The water had been much rougher than antici-
pated. So Bob started following the shoreline much closer
than usual when the propellor struck a rock hidden just
below the surface. The motor cut off and the boat drifted
onto the rock. He was stuck! Fortunately, a fisherman came

15

along and dragged the boat off the rock. The mangled pro-pellor somehow managed to crawl the boat to safety.

Striking rocks is a very common occurrence in the St. Lawrence River. But striking a rock in the middle of the desert is not. Yet, that is exactly what the Lord told Moses to do. And when he did, streams of water poured from the rock as God's provision to his thirsty people. He was also providing them with a prophetic symbol of the ultimate spiritual thirst-quencher soon to follow. The Apostle Paul wrote, "for they drank from the spiritual rock that accompanied them, and that rock was Christ." Striking a rock is not suggested to seaway travelers. But inviting Jesus Christ to accompany us on this earthly journey guarantees us a future that is truly Rock-solid.

## Waterlines

# 9. Defeating Goliath

Illustration courtesy U.S. Fish & Wildlife Service

> *All those gathered here will know that it is*
> *not by sword or spear that the LORD saves;*
> *for the battle is the LORD's.*
> *(1 Sam. 17:47)*

## River Cruise

*Read 1 Samuel 17:32–50*

## River Reflections

I was standing in the water up to my knees. I looked into the clear water and watched as a small sunfish swam up to me. He appeared to be investigating this giant intrusion into his fish-space. "Well, hello there, little guy" I said as he moved closer, seemingly unaware that I could have reached down and snatched him out of the water at any moment. He hovered in place, now poised just inches from my leg. Suddenly, he bolted forward and popped me on the ankle. Mind you, being attacked by a killer sunfish is about as painful as being hit with a marshmallow. Nevertheless, I was so shocked by his bold assault that I jumped out of the water and decided to do any further sunfish watching from the dock.

My fearless little shark-wannabe sunfish reminded me of the Biblical character, David, when he took on the mighty nine-foot tall Goliath. David wasn't thinking about the physical differences between them, nor was he concerned about the odds against him in such a mismatched conflict. All David saw was an arrogant man standing before him mocking his God. He boldly confronted Goliath saying, "You come against me with sword and spear and javelin, but I come against you in the name of the LORD Almighty" (1 Sam. 17:45). David ended up defeating the mighty Goliath with one small stone, a slingshot and a very big faith. Like David (and ferocious fish), it's not how big you are that counts. Victory comes down to being properly equipped. When we wield God's shield of faith, no Goliath is too big— no giant too powerful for us to defeat. In fact, with that kind of power, I might even be tempted to square off with that sunfish again some time.

## Waterlines

## 10. Known By Their Call

*We . . . will cry out to you in our distress,*
*and you will hear us and save us.*
*(2 Chron. 20:9)*

### River Cruise
*Read Psalm 139:1–16*

### River Reflections

My husband and I were snuggled together on the swinging
deck chair enjoying the peacefulness of a River evening. The
sun had already set but the sky was still ablaze with color.
Suddenly, the haunting two-noted cry of a loon pierced the
evening air. It was a sound we knew well and loved, and we
listened in wonder until the short concert subsided. The loon
is, without a doubt, my favorite of all waterfowl. There is no
sound on earth more enchanting. The Common Loon (or
Gavia Immer) is a beautiful large diving bird with distinctive
black and white plumage. But what is most distinctive about
the loon is its calls. While most are familiar with its two-note
wails, it also has three other calls: tremolos, hoots, and yodels.
The tremolos are what some describe as the laugh of the
loon. The hoot is a one-note call used between family mem-
bers. The yodel is the most complex sound and is used only

by the males. Researchers have discovered that the yodel is different for each bird and can therefore be used to identify individual loons. They refer to it as a verbal fingerprint or signature.

Researchers can know an individual loon by its call. Our Heavenly Father knows every individual person by our call, as well. We are told, "O LORD, you have searched me and you know me" (Ps. 139:1). But he desires to do so much more. The Bible assures us that even before we call he knows every thought we have and "Before a word is on my tongue you know it completely, O LORD" (Ps. 139:4). God knows our needs even before we call. He is just waiting for us to make that call so he can answer. So what are you waiting for?

## Waterlines

# 11. The Water Cycle

*Do you know how the clouds hang poised, those wonders of him who is perfect in knowledge?*
*(Job 37:16)*

## River Cruise
*Read Job 36:22–33*

## River Reflections

I do realize the River we love so much isn't the only beautiful body of water in the world. There are countless other magnificent lakes, oceans, seas and ponds as well. In addition to its waters, God has set up a complete hydraulic system here on earth that includes evaporation, cloud formation and precipitation. This system even includes the earth's weather patterns. The entire system is known as the earth's water cycle. Enormous quantities of water are lifted thousands of feet into the air through evaporation. They remain suspended there, held in place by hot air rising from the surface. The cooling air supports the water vapor in the clouds until the drops become large and heavy enough to fall back to the earth in the form of rain. The earth's waters also directly affect the weather patterns worldwide. Most of the water that forms into clouds comes from the oceans, that cover

70% of the earth's surfaces. So it is primarily the oceans that dictate the weather that produce the life-sustaining rains the earth needs planet-wide.

It has only been recently that scientists have come to understand the earth's complex water cycle. Yet, the Bible had described it quite accurately in one of its earliest books. The Book of Job, written thousands of years B.C., reveals a detailed description of the hydrological system of evaporation, clouds and rain. We read, "He draws up the drops of water, which distill as rain to the streams; the clouds pour down their moisture and abundant showers fall on mankind". Certainly, this wasn't something Job's contemporaries were aware of. No, this description of the earth's water cycle reaffirms both the accuracy and the Divine inspiration of the Scriptures. This yet-to-be discovered truth could only have been provided by the Master Engineer, himself.

## Waterlines

## 12. Pro-Creation

*'Where were you when I laid the earth's foundation?"*
*(Job 38:4)*

### River Cruise
*Read Job 38:4–7, 25–37*

### River Reflections
It began at around 2:00 A.M. I listened for a few moments by myself before elbowing my sleeping husband. "Bob! Wake up!" I whispered. Bob sprang up in bed. "Just listen" I said, hoping, now that I'd completely ruined his night's sleep, he'd appreciate what I woke him up for. Through our open window we could hear a continual loud splashing noise coming from the back bay out behind our camp. The splashing went on, uninterrupted, throughout the night. Bob guessed it was some kind of mammal like a beaver. I was betting on giant water monsters. Whatever it was, it was obviously big enough that we decided to wait until daylight to investigate. Early the next morning we went down to the water. To our amazement, we saw the fins of several huge fish cutting through the water. We discovered that the noise we had been hearing all night was that of carp spawning in the shallow water of the back bay.

We watched in awe as their giant bodies broke the surface as they performed their annual ritual of procreation.

Or, shall I say, Pro-Creation? As we gazed at the elegant water ballet taking place before us I couldn't help but to think of the Master choreographer who created each player in this dramatic performance. Some people believe that these graceful nuptial dancers came into existence by nothing more than mere chance. To these people the Lord asks, "Where were you when I laid the earth's foundation? . . . Have you journeyed to the springs of the sea or walked in the recesses of the deep? . . . Have you comprehended the vast expanses of the earth? Tell me, if you know all this" (Job 38:4,16–18). I wasn't there either, but I've seen enough of his handiwork to take him at his word.

## Waterlines

## 13. Heron Sense

*The stork . . . treats her young harshly, as if they were not hers; she cares not that her labor was in vain, for God did not endow her with wisdom or give her a share of good sense.*
*(Job 39:16,17)*

### River Cruise
*Read Job 39:13–30*

### River Reflections

On a warm summer night it sounds like a jungle as hundreds of Great Blue Herons sit and cackle on their island nests across from our camp. These giant stork-like bluish-grey birds stand anywhere from 40 to 52 inches and have a wingspan of over five feet. While it is impressive in appearance with its majestic long neck and stilt-like legs, survival for the heron is not easy. Female herons lay three to seven eggs in the spring but many of the young will not live past the second month. The adult brings food to the nest and the largest chicks immediately take the largest share. The smaller and less aggressive chicks grow steadily weaker and often fall from the nest as they are pushed aside by the others. Once they have fallen, they will face a swift death since the parents will not feed their young outside of the nest. Out of the three to seven eggs only two or three will reach adulthood.

Job describes the plight of the young ostrich or stork explaining that God did not equip its mother with "good sense." Instead, the adults instinctively allow the weaker chicks to go hungry, fall from the nest and die. But while God did not give them sense, he did amply provide for the herons' survival. In his perfectly balanced kingdom he designed the heron to produce enough eggs for the species to survive and thrive. And in God's economy even death has its place in providing food for other creatures. Unlike herons, God gave us humans good sense and with it, a responsibility. He has given us the assignment of caring for his kingdom and doing our best to protect each of his living creatures until he returns to bring true peace on earth.

## Waterlines

# 14. Planted By the Water

*He is like a tree planted by streams of water, which yields its fruit in season and whose leaf does not wither. Whatever he does prospers.*
*(Ps. 1:3)*

## River Cruise
Read Psalm 1:1–6

## River Reflections
I didn't get married right out of college as many of my friends did. I attended more weddings back then, than I can count. After a while I became convinced it would never be me walking down that aisle in white. I admit at times I struggled with that thought and found myself wrestling with the issue in prayer. If marriage wasn't for me, then what did the Lord have in mind for my life? If I wasn't supposed to share my life with someone special wouldn't I be terribly lonely? At that time I was living in a cottage on a small lake. It was there, at the end of the dock, where the Lord gave me the answer I needed to my questions.

I would often sit on the dock late at night and pour my heart out to God. Sometimes I would share my praises. At other times, my tears. I talked with him while gazing across the tranquil black waters as the starlight danced on its surface. As I did, my mind was lifted off my problems and my heart would dance with resounding joy. Anyone who has experienced this joy, the joy of sharing one's deepest thoughts with the Lord, also knows they need never fear loneliness. Nor do they need to doubt the wonderful plan this loving Father has for their life. I was living by the lake, planted by the water. I also discovered what it means to be planted in Jesus, the Living Water. Many years later the Lord brought someone special into my life, someone who also knew the joy of the Lord. I love my husband dearly but I am so thankful I found the joy first. Actually, there at the end of the dock, the joy found me.

## Waterlines

# 15. The Storm

*Out of the brightness of his presence clouds advanced,*
*with hailstones and bolts of lightning.*
*(Ps. 18:12)*

## River Cruise
*Read Psalm 18:1–19*

## River Reflections

Just after we were engaged, my parents decided to welcome
Bob into the family by taking us on a boat ride. It was a perfect day with not a cloud in the sky. Bob was new to the River
and was duly awed by its beauty. My parents made excellent
tour guides. They wove the boat around the many islands
describing each one by name. We had only been out for
about an hour when, to my surprise, my father abruptly
turned the boat around and headed toward home. My mom
nodded in agreement and announced, "We need to get back.
A storm is coming." Sure enough, when I looked to the north
I saw a wall of darkness on the horizon. It took less than 15
minutes to get back but the storm arrived just as we did. The
still water transformed almost instantaneously into a churn-
ing sea of whitecaps. The downpour quickly followed. Great
swelling waves battered the little boat which we quickly

hoisted out of the water. Apparently, my parents had gone through this before.

The Psalmist must have also experienced the power of such a storm. In Psalm 18, David eloquently describes the darkness, clouds, thunder and lightening, and even hailstones but then concludes, "He reached down from on high and took hold of me; he drew me out of deep waters" (18:16). David was in serious danger from enemies who were seeking his life. He used the illustration of the storm as a poetic way of saying that the Lord delivered him from them all. He added, "He rescued me because he delighted in me" (18:19). So next time you feel like you are being battered by the storms of life remember our God is in the rescue business because he delights in you.

## Waterlines

# 16. Sanctuary

*He makes me lie down in green pastures, he leads me
beside quiet waters, he restores my soul.*
*(Ps. 23:2, 3)*

## River Cruise
*Read Psalm 23:1–6*

## River Reflections
Back while Bob and I were first dating, we decided to take a
rowboat ride together. We had figured that going out on the
water and leisurely rowing around would be a relaxing way to
get to know each other better in a peaceful setting. At first, it
was anything but peaceful. There was a major festival going
on at the public beach. Power boats and water skiers raced
by us continually pummeling our little boat with their giant
wakes. Not great for rowing. There were several bands playing at the beach and the cacophony of their pounding
rhythms carried loudly across the water. Not great for chat-
ting either. We rowed past the beach and into a small back
bay. As Bob rowed farther into the bay we quickly found ourselves in another world. The thickly forested surroundings
completely muffled the din of the crowds and music, and the
water was still as glass. We felt as though we had been trans-

ported to some remote place on the Amazon. We let the boat freely float, enjoying the sounds of birds and the occasional croak of a frog. We talked freely and uninterrupted. We had discovered sanctuary.

I'm pretty sure David didn't have to contend with power boats or rock bands. But he was, no doubt, sitting in his own place of nature's sanctuary when he wrote the beloved words, "He leads me beside quiet waters." The Psalmist didn't live a life of ease and seclusion, however. He describes how he has faced enemies, evil, and even death. But the Psalmist was not afraid. He had found his place of sanctuary. Not just some lovely spot by the quiet waters. He wrote, "I will dwell in the house of the LORD forever." David found his sanctuary in the Lord.

## Waterlines

# 17. River of Delights

*They feast on the abundance of your house; you give them drink from your river of delights.*
*(Ps. 36:8)*

## River Cruise
*Read Psalm 36:1–12*

## River Reflections
It was "pick your favorite hymn" night at church. I sat on the piano bench and looked out at the small but vibrant gathering seated before me. Not a big group on this cold winter night, but the joy in their faces seemed to melt away the winter chill. The song leader could barely keep up with them as they called out song after song. "Okay, we have time for just one more" he finally managed to interject. An elderly man near the back called out his request. I remember seeing tears on his cheeks as the group rose to their feet and sang, "Like a river glorious is God's perfect peace. Over all victorious in its bright increase. Perfect, yet it floweth, fuller every day. Perfect, yet it groweth deeper all the way." Surely, this man who had walked so many years with the Lord had, indeed, seen God's perfect peace growing deeper and fuller in his own life . . . like a river, glorious.

In Psalm 36, the Psalmist also writes about a river, referring to it as a "river of delights." But what was he trying to describe? What is the river of delights that the Lord gives us to drink from? This song actually began as a cry of frustration over the seemingly unchecked sinfulness of evil men. But David abruptly shifts gears and lifts his focus upward to the Lord saying, "Your love, O LORD, reaches to the heavens, your faithfulness to the skies." God pours his love on us like a fountain of sparkling, living water. The river of delights is the unfailing love of God and he gives it in abundance to all who come to him and ask. The Psalmist ends his song in victory knowing God's love will ultimately triumph over evil.

## Waterlines

## 18. There is a River

*There is a river, whose streams make glad the city of God, the holy place where the most high dwells.*
*(Ps. 46:4)*

### River Cruise
*Read Psalm 46:1–11*

### River Reflections
We sat side-by-side on the dock swinging our legs over the water. We had only been married a few months and I was feeling blissfully in love on this beautiful day. After a while, Bob looked and noticed I was crying. "What's wrong?" he asked worriedly. I blurted out how sad I was that we wouldn't be married in Heaven, and that we wouldn't even be able to enjoy the River there. It took several years before Bob quit trying to figure out what triggered such emotional outbursts. Despite his confusion, he reminded me of what we do know about Heaven and the indescribable glory that awaits us there. The Bible refers to Heaven as Paradise, a place without any sorrow or tears, that is beyond our comprehension and our greatest expectations. But best of all, it is the place where we will be eternally reunited with Jesus.

That evening, a verse I had read many times before seemed to leap off the page. "There is a river . . . " Suddenly it hit me. Who ever said God's Heaven wouldn't have a river? And if the rivers here on earth could be so lovely, how much more beautiful would the river be in his heavenly home! Would the God who created this earth and said "It is good" not design a heavenly paradise of which he could say, "It is much better"? Similarly, if the union to one person (like my beloved Bob) could be so wonderful, imagine being eternally joined with him, all the other believers, *and* the Lord, himself. Yes, there is a River up there in Heaven awaiting me. Even better, there is a Savior who loved me enough to save a place there for me, for Bob, and for all who have entrusted their lives to him.

## Waterlines

# 19. Driftwood

Photo by Upsilon Andromedae

*For you, O God, tested us; you refined us like silver . . . we went through fire and water, but you brought us to a place of abundance.*
*(Ps. 66:10–12)*

## River Cruise
*Read Psalm 66:1–20*

## River Reflections

It was my first trip out on the River for the season. It was also the perfect time of year for finding driftwood. I followed the shoreline closely searching intently until I spotted what I was looking for. "It is perfect", I thought to myself, and with some difficulty I managed to drag it into the boat. What some might have considered nothing more than a useless chunk of dead wood I saw as a potential masterpiece. I headed home with my treasure victoriously. Then, the real work began. I had grown up watching my mom rescue pieces of driftwood and then turn them into works of art. It took her months of labor, drying, sanding and polishing but the end product was always well worth the effort. Our home and yard were adorned with my mom's beautiful finished works of art.

Yes, refinishing driftwood is a time consuming venture. It takes a lot of energy, skill, and commitment to turn a piece of discarded wood into a valuable piece of art. But it is worth the effort. Thankfully, God felt the same way about us. Like the driftwood, we humans were lost, floating aimlessly along as good as dead in our sins. But God saw a potential masterpiece in each of us. So he came to earth to rescue us. Those who hopped onboard, he began to carefully, lovingly refinish and turn them into a work of art. It is true that the restoration process can be painful at times while he sands away the rough spots. But the end product is not only worth His effort. It is miraculous. As the song goes, "I once was lost, but now am found." By his amazing grace I am on my way to becoming one of his masterpieces.

## Waterlines

# 20. "Fragrant Bean"

*Though you have made me see troubles, many and bitter, you will restore my life again; from the depths of the earth you will again bring me up.*

*(Ps. 71:20)*

## River Cruise
*Read Psalm 71:1–24*

## River Reflections

It was one of the most stunningly beautiful wooden boats Bob and I had ever seen. We learned that the Mokihana was a 40-foot mahogany cruiser built in 1987 in Venice, Italy. It was made of a unique, unstained mahogany wood taken from just two trees so the grain could be perfectly matched from top to bottom. It was a spotless, glossy wooden boat in pristine condition inside and out. We learned that the Mokihana had recently gone through a complete transformation process. Originally purchased by a hotel in Kauai as a water taxi, it was given its name which means "Fragrant Bean" in Hawaiian. After a few years the hotel went bankrupt and the Mokihana was abandoned and left to rot. Five years later it was discovered by an antique boat collector who purchased it for a dollar and restored the decaying boat to its original condition.

Like the Mokihana, each of us was masterfully crafted but because sin had entered the world we were rendered spiritually bankrupt. Though we had been made in the glorious image of our Maker we were now covered with decay. Apart from some kind of intervention, we were abandoned and left without hope. But someone who happened to have a Designer's eye for beauty did intervene. We were purchased, not for a dollar but with God's own life. He then began the restoration process taking what was rotten and exchanging it with "the aroma of Christ . . . the fragrance of life" (2 Cor. 2:16). After being restored, the Mokihana was disassembled and transported to its new home on the River. Each of us will one day be disassembled and leave these earthly bodies behind. Those of us who belong to Christ will be transported to our new home on his River of Life.

## Waterlines

## 21. Evening Worship

*The sea is his, for he made it, and his hands formed the dry land. Come, let us bow down in worship, let us kneel before the LORD our Maker.*

*(Ps. 95:5–6)*

### River Cruise
*Read Psalm 95:1–11*

### River Reflections

Someone once asked me if I could name a favorite worship service I had been to. At first, I couldn't answer. I have had the wonderful opportunity to worship in all kinds of churches from Baptist to Pentecostal, with worship styles ranging from old-fashioned hymn sings to drum sets and dancing. Did I have a favorite? Do I prefer one over the other? There were aspects I have come to appreciate about every different style (well, *almost* every style). As I debated the strengths of each, an entirely different worship service came to mind. There was, indeed, one time of worship I had experienced that stood out from all the others.

I had just gotten home from an exhausting and demanding day. I hopped in my kayak and headed out on the water. I paddled out into the middle of the River and, since there was no wind, just let the boat drift. I took a deep breath of the fresh air and finally felt truly relaxed. My mind drifted off and I lost track of time as the sun edged toward the horizon. I decided I would enjoy the sunset before heading back to shore. I watched as the sun slowly slipped down behind the lush, tree-lined shore. The quiet waters lapped gently against the side of the boat beckoning me to linger just a few more moments. I looked up into the sky and noticed the fading light had set the puffy white clouds on fire. A brilliant yellow/orange reflected back from the shimmering waters. I was suddenly overcome by the artistry manifesting itself before me and tears began to freely flow down my cheeks. I found myself worshiping as I had never done before. My spontaneous worship service required only an audience of One; the Creator.

## Waterlines

# 22. Morning Praise

*Sing to the LORD, praise his name; proclaim his salvation day after day.*
*(Ps. 96:2)*

## River Cruise
*Read Psalm 96:1–13*

## River Reflections

My husband and I used to have the unique opportunity during the summer months of going to church on an island. Sunday services were held at Jorstadt Castle (now Singer Castle) on Dark Island in the Thousand Islands since the 1960's, were open to the public, but were only accessible by boat. We would make the journey across the mighty St. Lawrence Seaway to participate in this delightful worship experience. We would arrive each week to join a group of our fellow boaters in bringing our praises to the Lord. It didn't hurt a bit that regardless of where one sat in the chapel, one was guaranteed a full view of the River. Perhaps that is, in part, why the singing was always so dynamic and rich. Looking out over some of the most magnificent works of God's hands indeed helps inspire one to lift one's voice in praise to the One who made it all.

I have the feeling the Psalmist could relate to the experience we had at Jorstadt. Surely he knew what it meant to be inspired by creation when he urged his listeners to sing to the Lord and to "Ascribe to the LORD the glory due his name" (Ps. 96:2). As his song continues he declares, "Let the heavens rejoice, let the earth be glad; let the sea resound, and all that is in it; let the fields be jubilant, and everything in them. Then all the trees of the forest will sing for joy; they will sing before the LORD . . ." (Ps. 96:11–13). The Psalmist is not only writing a praise song to the Lord about his creation. He is actually describing creation singing praise to its Creator. In fact, when we sing our praises to him, we are but adding our voices to the rest of creation as it declares the glory of the Lord. Knowing we are a part of that praise team gives us all the more to sing about.

## Waterlines

## 22. Sea Psalms

> *Let the sea resound, and everything in it,*
> *the world, and all who live in it.*
> *Let the rivers clap their hands. . . .*
> *(Ps. 98:7, 8)*

### River Cruise
Read Psalm 98:1–9

### River Reflections
Having a camp directly on the River has allowed me to experience the many moods of water. Almost like human emotions, it can be peaceful, bright and cheerful while at other times it becomes turbulent, raging and dark. The Book of Psalms describes the many moods of water. We can read about the quiet waters, or how those same waters writhe and convulse. Water is even described as an instrument of praise. But the Psalms have much more to say about the emotions of humans. Within this one book the full range of human passions are expressed from the depths of despair to the heights of ecstasy. Whatever we are feeling, we can come to the Psalms and find that others have gone through these very same emotions. We can also find reassurance that those who have, found comfort in God. He understands our emotions not just because he made them but because he became a

man, and experienced them, himself. In fact, some of the most passionate words in the Psalms were the prophetic cries of the Messiah who cried, "My God, my God, why have you forsaken me?" (Ps. 22:1) as he was crucified on our behalf.

But the Psalms aren't just about negative emotions. Despair is far outweighed by words of triumph and victorious shouts of praise. Even the Psalm that began with the cries of the Messiah ended in the victorious cry, "for he has done it". Because of Christ's victory on the Cross the child of God is assured of the victory over every sorrow, sin, and death. So, come to the water if you want to experience its many moods. But when you are having moods of your own, good or bad, come to the Psalms. There, you can experience God.

## Waterlines

# 24. Creation Song

*He wraps himself in light as with a garment; he stretches out the heavens like a tent and lays the beams of his upper chambers on their waters.*

(Ps. 104:2, 3)

## River Cruise
Read Psalm 104:1–35

## River Reflections
Perhaps you thought the only creation account in the Bible was "In the beginning." Various accounts of God as the creator of all things are found throughout the Scriptures. But few passages are written as eloquently as Psalm 104. The Psalmist offers his version of the creation story in the form of a praise song. Indeed, God's work of creation is worthy of our praise. The author begins by directing his song to the Creator himself exclaiming, "Praise the LORD, O my soul. O LORD my God, you are very great; you are clothed with splendor and majesty." Truly, before anything else existed, there was God. Then, there was light. Then he created the Universe. Then, to the delight of us River-lovers, God created the waters and used them to water every living thing on earth. We read, "He makes springs pour water into the ravines; it flows between the mountains. They give water to all the

beasts of the field; the wild donkeys quench their thirst. The birds of the air nest by the waters; they sing among the branches . . . the earth is satisfied by the fruit of his work."

After everything else was in order, the Psalmist mentions humans saying, "Then man goes out to his work, to his labor until evening." God provided a world full of beauty and living things, and then placed us here to live and work in this marvelous place. In the final strains of his song, the Psalmist acknowledges that mankind brought sin and imperfection to this otherwise perfect world. He humbly requests, "But may sinners vanish from the earth and the wicked be no more." Clearly, the Psalmist has absolute confidence that his Creator will one day honor this request. He ends as jubilantly as he began singing, "Praise the LORD."

## Waterlines

# 25. Range Lights

*Your word is a lamp to my feet*
*and a light for my path.*
*(Ps. 119:105)*

## River Cruise
*Read Psalm 119:97–112*

## River Reflections

We sat on the deck under a star-filled sky. The only sounds breaking the silence on this warm summer's eve was the gentle background music of the crickets. Bob heard it first, an almost inaudible droning in the distance. A ship was slowing making its way up the channel. Soon, the stream of its lights began to appear as it came into sight. The massive Seaway lakers are a visual feast as they travel down the River at night. But the beautiful lights serve a very practical purpose. By law, every ship must be lit according to marine standards. The starboard (right) side must have a green light while the port (left) side must have a red light. The bow (front) and stern (rear) each require a specifically placed light which, together, are called range lights. The two range lights help an oncoming vessel identify the ship's position and direction of travel. If the lights appear to be moving apart the range is opening indicating the boat is moving to the left or right. As they come together the range is closing meaning the ship is aiming straight ahead.

God's Word and his Holy Spirit have a role similar to that of range lights in the life of the believer. Together, they keep us directly on course. Like ships in the night, without some kind of guiding light in our lives, it is easy to drift off the right path. If we find ourselves off track or even if we temporarily lose our way, the light of God's Word combined with the illumination of his Spirit will guide us safely back. When we set our sights on these two guiding Lights we can go forward in the full assurance that we will ultimately reach our destination and safe harbor.

## Waterlines

_____

_____

_____

_____

_____

_____

_____

_____

_____

_____

_____

_____

_____

_____

_____

## 26. Heron Dance

*My mouth will speak in praise of the LORD. Let every creature praise his holy name for ever and ever.*
(Ps. 145:21)

### River Cruise
*Read Psalm 145:1–21*

### River Reflections
One could almost imagine the flowing sounds of a symphony playing somewhere in the background. The calm air was filled with the late summer sounds of crickets, locusts and chirping birds. A gentle haze formed over the water giving it an ethereal appearance. As we watched, a Great Blue Heron entered into the tranquil scene before us. It flew slowly across the water, high at first but then descending toward the surface. The giant bird dipped down with its legs outstretched as if to settle on the water but just before touching the surface it pulled back up. We then noticed another heron flying in from the left. It, too, dipped down almost grazing the surface then lifting majestically back into the air. The two graceful creatures continued in this steady cycle flowing down and rising back into the air in contrasting motions. As we watched in silent wonder there seemed to be no practical purpose to

their flight patterns. No, they looked more like a dance troupe giving a command performance. And indeed they were. The herons were performing a ballet of praise to an audience of one.

The Scriptures affirm that every living thing gives glory to God. Not just here on earth, but in Heaven as well. We are given a brief glimpse through a vision given to John who wrote, "Then I heard every creature in heaven and on earth and under the earth and on the sea, and all that is in them, singing: 'To him who sits on the throne and to the Lamb be praise and honor and glory and power, for ever and ever!'" (Rev. 5:13). Truly, all of creation gives witness to the Creator. In fact, some even dance. And by the way, I still think I heard music playing . . . somewhere.

## Waterlines

# 27. Reflections

*As water reflects a face, so a man's*
*heart reflects the man.*
*(Prov. 27:19)*

## River Cruise
*Read Proverbs 29:1–19*

## River Reflections

What can I say? God made me emotional. Sometimes I consider my intense emotions a gift. At times, however, they
seem more like a curse. After overreacting to a difficult situation one day, I headed to my favorite place by the water to
talk with the Lord about it. At first, I sat quietly, simply taking
in the beauty and was struck by how perfectly calm the water
was. I could see an exact mirrored reflection of the islands
across the channel. Every detail was clearly visible in the picture reflecting off the water. As I watched, however, the image
began to slightly blur. A breeze had stirred the waters and the
blur began to spread across the River. As it did, the formerly
perfect reflection became marred and distorted. The wind
continued to pick up until finally no reflection was visible at
all. All that remained was gray, choppy water.

I saw a reflection of my own life in the water that day. When I am focused on the Lord my emotions remain steady and I reflect his image to others. When I take my eyes off of him, the turbulent waves of my own emotions completely blur the image of the One I want to reflect. We are told to, "Be still and know I am God" (Ps. 46:10). It is only by resting in him, that he can be reflected in me. The only responsibility of the one doing the reflecting is to be still before the object being reflected. He who calms the raging seas is only waiting for us to cease from our own anxious labors and rest in him. He can calm our troubled hearts, fill us with his peace and allow others to get a glimpse of his glory reflected in us.

## Waterlines

_____

_____

_____

_____

_____

_____

_____

_____

_____

_____

_____

_____

_____

_____

_____

## 28. Zebulun

*Nevertheless, there will be no more gloom for those who were in distress. In the past he humbled the land of Zebulun and the land of Naphtali, but in the future he will honor Galilee of the Gentiles, by the way of the sea, along the Jordan."*

(Is. 9:1)

### River Cruise
*Read Matthew 4:1–16*

### River Reflections

Jesus must have loved the water. As he walked the shores of Galilee, shores that he created, I wonder if he ever just stopped and gazed at its beauty and thought, as he had long before, "It is good!" We do know he spent a lot of time there. In fact, we knew he would do so, even before his birth. When Jacob blessed each of his 12 sons he prophesied that Zebulun would "live by the seashore and become a haven for ships" (Gen. 49:13). As prophesied, when Israel entered the Promised Land, the tribe of Zebulun settled down by the Sea of Galilee. Isaiah prophesied that the promised Messiah would begin his ministry in the land of Zebulun. And it was there by the Sea of Galilee that Jesus called his first disciples. Jesus' earthy ministry began by the sea; it also ended there. After his death and resurrection Jesus told his disciples to "go to Galilee; there they will see me" (Mt. 28:10). There, he gave them their final instructions before returning to the Father. Surely, the shores of Galilee must hold a special place in his heart.

There by the sea Jesus' earthly ministry came to an end. His parting words, however, assured his followers that his ministry to the earth had just begun. Empowered by his Spirit, they would carry the message of his love and salvation from the shores of Galilee to every shore on the earth. Then, once they carried his Good News to the entire world, he promised he would return for them, in person. Yes, he who formed the Sea of Galilee, placed Zebulun on its shores, and walked those shores himself, will no doubt be walking those shores again some day soon. Maybe we'll walk them together.

## Waterlines

# 29. Daylight Savings

*The people walking in darkness have seen a great light; on those living in the land of the shadow of death a light has dawned.*

*(Is. 9:2)*

## River Cruise
*Read Isaiah 8:21–9:7*

## River Reflections

Tonight we will be setting our clocks back for the winter season. For me, this annual event never passes without a feeling of sadness. I watched earlier this evening as the sun slowly dipped behind the hills with one last blaze of glory. I continued to gaze out the window trying to savor every last moment of lingering light as it reflected off the water's rippling surface. Even the brilliant autumn reds and oranges of the trees in the background eventually faded into the grayness of the evening. It felt as though another season had just gone to bed. Plus, I know that for the next six months when I leave work each night I will be entering a world of darkness.

I admittedly get a little dramatic about the one hour shift away from Daylight Savings Time. For me, it means that those sunsets by the water I enjoy so much will have been moved just out of my reach. It is interesting that the Christmas season falls at the time when the days are shortest and the darkness the greatest. The Prophet Isaiah described the spiritual darkness of the world before Christ was born saying, "Then they will look toward the earth and see only distress and darkness and fearful gloom, and they will be thrust into utter darkness" (Is. 8:22). The Messiah's arrival would be like a spiritual Daylight Savings Time. Isaiah wrote that the people in darkness would see a great Light. He then identified that light as the "Wonderful Counselor, Mighty God, Everlasting Father, Prince of Peace" (Is. 9:6). The days will soon be getting longer as we approach the return of Daylight Savings Time. What is even more exciting is that we will one day see the return of Isaiah's Great Light, Jesus.

## Waterlines

# 30. Ships in the Night

*Whether you turn to the right or to the left, your
ears will hear a voice behind you, saying,
"This is the way; walk in it.
(Is. 30:21)*

## River Cruise
Read Isaiah 30:15–21

## River Reflections

It was our first vacation on the River and after a day full of
adventures we had gone to bed exhausted. In the middle of
the night I was awakened by the blast of a horn. A few
moments later another horn sounded from the opposite
direction. "Ships!" I shouted and jumped out of bed heading,
pajamas and all, for the back door. Having gotten to the
porch just ahead of me, my mother looked as excited as I
was. We stood side-by-side and watched the two brightly lit
tankers pass each other in the dark waters. Years later, I find
myself no less enthralled by the sound of ship horns in the
night. I have since learned that each horn blast has a meaning
and is a form of communication between ships. One long
blast indicates that the ship intends to pass the oncoming
vessel on the right. The oncoming vessel then (hopefully)
returns the same message. Two long blasts are for passing

on the left. By signals like these the captain doesn't need to guess the other ship's intent. The message is perfectly clear.

In a dark world of shifting standards and the abandonment of moral absolutes, choosing the right direction can be difficult at times, and the path unclear. Yet, God's truth remains firm. Like a ship's horn the Bible is his loud and clear way of signaling his intent and communicating his directions. It warns us of danger. He also uses it to let us know if we have veered to the left or the right, and to guide us back on track. If we seek his direction in our lives, he will make his intent known to us. Through his Holy Spirit and his Word he will make the way perfectly clear.

## Waterlines

_____

_____

_____

_____

_____

_____

_____

_____

_____

_____

_____

_____

_____

_____

_____

# 31. The Morning Mist

> *I have swept away your offenses like a cloud, your sins like the morning mist. Return to me, for I have redeemed you.*
>
> (Is. 44:22)

## River Cruise
Read Isaiah 44:9–26

## River Reflections
I felt grumpy when I heard them forecasting the first frost of the season. To me, frost was a sign of the inevitable—that summer was now behind us, and that winter was just around the corner. We would be closing camp for the season, the River would soon be frozen over and I would be spending next several long, cold, dark months awaiting the spring thaw and our return to the River. The next morning, I went to the window to assess the damage. As predicted, a fine white frost covered our entire backyard. What caught my attention, however, was the far more exotic sight just beyond it. The River was completely engulfed in a thick mist lifting itself from the water's surface. The warm water temperature colliding with the freezing temperatures had created this surreal sight before me. I stood memorized at the window as the first rays of morning light began to illuminate the mist over the water and the effect was absolutely enchanting.

In less than an hour, it was gone. The bright morning sunlight had completely burned off the mist and the frost with not a trace to be seen. Such is the light of God's love for each of us. When we allow unconfessed sins to build up in our lives, they cover us like a thick mist. They act as barriers, blocking out our ability to freely experience God's love for us, as well as the ability of that love to shine through us to others. The very moment, however, that we expose those sins to God's forgiving grace by confessing them to him, he melts them away like the morning mist. I excitedly grabbed my jacket and headed out the door. It's going to be a beautiful day, after all.

## Waterlines

# 32. Called By Name

> *I will give you the treasures of darkness, riches*
> *stored in secret places, so that you will know that*
> *I am the Lord . . . I summon you by name*
> *and bestow on you a title of honor.*
> *(Is. 45:3, 4)*

## River Cruise
*Read Isaiah 43:1–12*

## River Reflections

I have always loved to watch the ships as they continually cruise by our camp. So does my dad. In fact, he keeps a book by his chair called, "Know Your Ships" in which he has kept meticulous records of every ship he had seen making a mark by its name along with the date he had seen it and the direction it was headed. His notes revealed he had even sometimes seen the same ship on its return trip down the River. As I read, I also discovered for myself how to determine the name, company, and country of origin of every ship. The stack of the ship reveals its company logo. The flag hung at the stern of the vessel is the national flag of the country in which it is registered. If a different flag is being flown at the bow, it is most likely the national flag of the port it is visiting. The ship's name is printed on its bow and also across the stern along with its port of registry. Knowing that, it is no wonder my dad was often able to identify a ship by name.

As amazing as my dad's knowledge of ships is, it cannot be compared to God's knowledge about each of us. Imagine that! The Creator of the Universe not only intimately knows us, but actually calls us by name. The ships on the seaway are used to transport valuable cargos. God has given his children the privilege of transporting of a far greater treasure. He has called us, by name, to take the riches of his love to a needy world. He will one day call each of us back to our Port of Hail where a new name, a title of honor, awaits us.

## Waterlines

## 33. Peace Like A River

> *If only you had paid attention to my commands,*
> *your peace would have been like a river,*
> *your righteousness like the waves of the sea.*
> *(Is. 48:18)*

### River Cruise
*Read Isaiah 48:12–22*

### River Reflections
If you were to ask me what I love so much about the River the first reason I would give (mind you, I could offer thousands) would be that it is so peaceful there. No matter how hectic the day, I can retreat to the water's edge and feel the pressures melt away. I don't think I ever claimed to have the niche on this liquid admiration but I was surprised, nevertheless, to find that the association of the water with peace was actually biblical. In trying to draw them back to himself God told his rebellious people, "My own hand laid the foundations of the earth, and my right hand spread out the heavens; when I summon them, they all stand up together" (Is. 48:13). He who made all things promised that if they would return to him, "your peace would have been like a river." Much to my delight I discovered that the Creator, himself, must feel

the same way I do about the water. And even better, it was he who designed it to be that way. Perhaps that is why so many of us who love the Creator also love the water.

In fact, you can pick up any hymnal and discover that quite a few of the hymn writers refer to water. And speaking of peace, how about lyrics like these? "I've got peace like a river . . . in my soul. I've got love like an ocean . . . in my soul. I've got joy like a fountain . . . in my soul." Truly, this fellow water-lover has discovered the ultimate Source for his peace. Yes, the water's edge is a very peaceful place to be. But the peace that passes all understanding is a permanent condition that remains in our hearts when the Author of peace abides there.

## Waterlines

# 34. Two Islands

*The Spirit of the Sovereign LORD is on me, because*
*the LORD has anointed me to preach good*
*news to the poor. He has sent me to . . .*
*to proclaim the year of the LORD's favor*
*and the day of vengeance of our God.*
(Is. 61:1, 2)

## River Cruise
*Read Isaiah 61:1–11*

## River Reflections

When my parents first told me they had purchased property on the River I was delighted. When they told me there was an island just across the channel I was ecstatic. I spent most of my first visit looking across the water at "our" island. I learned it was a state-owned bird sanctuary and I could even see the nests of the Great Blue Herons in the treetops. What I couldn't figure out was why there was a fancy looking private home on the far end of the island. It was almost a year later before the mystery was solved. Once we crossed the channel in our boat we discovered that we had actually been looking at two separate islands. One was the bird sanctuary but right in front of it was a smaller island with the private home. From our distant perspective, the two islands had appeared to be one. Only as we got closer could the two be distinguished from each other.

Isaiah prophesied of the coming Messiah. Hundreds of years later, Jesus got up to speak in the Temple and read from Isaiah 61. But after he read, "to proclaim the year of the LORD's favor" He stopped abruptly. The crowd stared, every eye fixed on him as he proclaimed, "Today this scripture is fulfilled in your hearing" (Lk. 4:21). Jesus was claiming to be the Messiah. But what about the rest of the verse? You see, Isaiah was actually speaking of two islands, two separate events involving the coming Messiah. From his distant perspective they appeared as one. When Jesus came he fulfilled the first part of the prophecy. When he comes again he will take those of us who are awaiting him to that lovely home he has been preparing on the second island.

## Waterlines

_____

_____

_____

_____

_____

_____

_____

_____

_____

_____

_____

_____

_____

_____

_____

# 35. Leaky Buckets

*My people have committed two sins: They have
forsaken me, the spring of living water, and
have dug their own cisterns, broken
cisterns that cannot hold water.*

*(Jer. 2:13)*

## River Cruise
Read Jeremiah 2:1–13, 24:7–8

## River Reflections
Why would I need a bailing bucket? My old rowboat simply
did not leak. So when I put it in the water for the season I
didn't bother with a bucket. Then it rained. And it rained,
and it rained, and when I next visited my waterproof boat,
there was over a foot of water in the bottom. I furtively
glanced over at the boat docked next to mine and spotted a
large plastic jug. I figured the owner wouldn't mind if I bor-
rowed it for a few minutes. However, as I lifted my first scoop
of water from the bottom of my boat the water poured right
back into the boat. The jug, I quickly realized, had two large
cracks running down its sides. I immediately arrived at the
conclusion that crime just doesn't pay. I was mortified to find
out that the marina owner had been observing my whole
ordeal. He came over carrying two large buckets and asked if

I needed any help. I meekly took him up on his offer and was seaworthy in a matter of minutes.

The Prophet Jeremiah used the illustration of broken cisterns to describe those who had forsaken God and were trying to make it through life doing things their own way. They could have had the Living Water but had chosen, instead, to try bailing themselves out with their own leaky buckets. Jeremiah was reminding them that even when we turn our backs on him, our God remains a God of grace. Like the marina owner, he is quietly watching as we attempt to do things our own way. But he is just waiting for our cry for help so he can come to our aid with his giant buckets of love. All we have to do is ask.

## Waterlines

# 36. The One That Got Away

Photo © Michael "Mike" L. Baird bairdphotos.com

*And the Lord commanded the fish, and it*
*vomited Jonah onto dry land.*
*(Jonah 2:10)*

## River Cruise
*Read Jonah 2:1–10*

## River Reflections

You might call it the ultimate fish story though it wasn't your
typical "man catches fish" tale. Rather, in this story, it was the
fish that caught the man. No, Jonah hadn't gone out looking
for a fish. He was actually running away from something, or,
shall we say, Someone. Having directly disobeyed God's
orders, Jonah was now trying to escape him by heading to the
high seas. However, even though he was running away from
God, Jonah hadn't stopped believing in him. When asked by
his fellow sailors who he was, Jonah responded, "I am a
Hebrew and I worship the Lord, the God of Heaven, who
made the sea and the land" (Jonah 1:9). Jonah also believed
that the storm that was about to destroy them all was due to
his disobedience. So he told the others to throw him overboard into the raging seas. Jonah probably thought he would

be paying the ultimate price for his sins. But he was willing to entrust his life into the hands of his Heavenly Father.

But the Lord had different plans for Jonah. He wanted to teach him a lesson in trust. He also wanted to give him a second chance. The Lord arranged for a giant fish to swallow Jonah alive and for three days Jonah had an uninterrupted quiet time with his God. Jonah repented of his sins and rededicated his life, such as it was in a fish's belly, to the Lord. But this fish story wasn't just about the one that got away. Actually, two got away that day. Not by accident, but by grace. Jonah had deserved being fish bait but instead received forgiveness and a second chance. As for the fish, I assume it was nothing a few antacids couldn't take care of.

## Waterlines

## 37. Son-Rise

> *But for you who revere my name, the sun
> of righteousness will rise with healing in
> its wings. And you will go out and leap
> like calves released from the stall.*
> *(Mal. 4:2)*

### River Cruise
*Read Malachi 3:16–4:5*

### River Reflections

It was the first day of vacation. We had gone to bed discussing all the possibilities for the next morning, but none of them included rain. It was so dark that when I first woke up I thought it was still night. However, glancing at my watch I quickly realized the day was well underway. Apparently, no one thought to notify the sun. I looked out over the water which appeared gray and colorless. Ruling out most of the other possibilities for the day, we opted, instead, to go into town and do some shopping. Four hours and several cheap souvenirs later the day hadn't improved a bit. We sat on the porch for the rest of the day until, according to our best estimations, the sun had set. Then we went to bed, hoping for a better day tomorrow.

Very early the next morning, I could sense light coming in the window. I jumped out of bed and ran to the deck just in time to see a burst of glorious light appear over the water. My heart filled with exhilaration as yesterday's gray and dismal world transformed before my eyes. The water reflected the sun's glow and the whole world seemed to come alive with vibrant color. It was going to be a great day! Suddenly, the verses in Isaiah came to mind "The people walking in darkness have seen a great light; on those living in the land of the shadow of death a light has dawned" (Is. 9:2). Malachi, too, described the coming Messiah as the rising of the Sun of Righteousness. In their lifetimes, they would not see Jesus appear on earth, nor would they experience the Son-rise, but under the inspiration of the Holy Spirit they couldn't have described it better.

## Waterlines

## 38. Dancing Lights

> *In the same way, let your light shine*
> *before men, that they may see your good*
> *deeds and praise your Father in heaven.*
> *(Mt. 5:16)*

### River Cruise
*Read Matthew 5:3–16*

### River Reflections

Once I get started I don't know when to stop. Whether I'm
catching anything is often irrelevant since what I love most
about fishing is the sun, the fresh air and the water. I had cast
my first line around mid-afternoon and was still at it several
hours later (though, if I remember correctly, I had run out of
worms some time ago). I hadn't even noticed that the sun
was beginning its final ascent. What caught my attention was
a stunningly brilliant pulsating motion that had begun to
take place on the water. The sun's rays were shining directly
on the delicately rippling surface making the waters appear as
though they were performing a dance of light. The sparkling
path appeared to stream from the far shore right to where I
was sitting. The glistening waters not only seemed alive but as
if they were dancing in praise of their Creator.

My fishing rod now totally forgotten, I was completely caught up in this dance of sunlight and water. While the sparkling water was what caught my attention, I realized it was the sun, not the water that created the light show. How perfectly that describes the Church! We are a reflection of God's light to the rest of the world. When people are drawn to God through his people, it is not because any of us are anything special or particularly attractive in, and of ourselves. No, what attracts people—what catches their eye is seeing God's light shining upon us and through us. God, himself, gets to enjoy that light in us as well. When we respond to God's love by lifting our praises to him, they are but a reflection of that love sparkling from us, back to him in a never-ending dance of light.

## Waterlines

# 39. The Beaufort Scale

*Come to me, all you who are weary and*
*burdened, and I will give you rest…*
*you will find rest for your souls.*
*(Mt. 11:28, 29)*

## River Cruise
*Read Matthew 11:20–30*

## River Reflections

Sometimes we humans seem to prefer learning things the
hard way. When it comes to safe boating, however, the hard
way can be disastrous. After a few harrowing experiences we
quickly learned to check the marine forecast *before* taking
our boat out on the water. The National Weather Service
provides current weather information 24 hours a day that
includes the wind velocity and wave height. Most marine
forecasts are based on the Beaufort Weather Scale which
assigns a particular level on a scale of 1 to 12 of wind conditions and wave height. A level 0 (or "calm") is a wind of 0–1
knots, and a wave height of 0 feet. As levels increase the wind
condition moves from calm, to light breeze, strong breeze,
gale, storm, and violent storm. At the top of the scale, level
12, with winds of 64 knots and wave heights of 45 feet or

more, is considered a hurricane. Probably not a good day for pleasure boating.

The Beaufort Scale reminds me of a stress level scale I'd once seen. Major traumas such as the death of a loved one or divorce caused the highest levels of stress while events such as changing jobs or moving were lower on the list. As the total number of points increase, one's stress level is likely to move from light breeze on up to a full blown emotional hurricane. One factor this scale fails to recognize is the effect one's faith can have on stress levels. Jesus promised to help carry our burdens and to provide rest for our weary souls. This is the very same Jesus who spoke a word, and calmed the raging seas. Even in life's most overwhelming situations, with him along in the boat, we can maintain a Beaufort level of 0.

## Waterlines

# 40. Red Sky At Night

*When evening comes, you say, "It will be fair weather, for the sky is red" and in the morning, "Today it will be stormy, for the sky is red and overcast."*

(Mt. 16:2, 3)

## River Cruise
*Read Matthew 15:29–16:3*

## River Reflections

"What we need here is a sign!" I was supposed to give a concert on an island the next day, weather permitting. But the weather wasn't looking very permitting. The forecasts were gloomy and the sky was an ominous gray. I had always heard, "Red sky at night, sailor's delight; red in the morning, sailor take warning" but thought to myself, "perhaps this time it is wrong." I got up early the next morning and began warming up my voice as a red sun rose over the horizon. But the wind was calm. Though I knew better, I secretly wished for some sign that we should go ahead and make the trip. Instead, true to all the signs we had already been given, the wind began to pick up. Within the next hour it reached near gale level. Had we been in the boat we would not have made it to church. Or back.

The religious leaders of the day asked Jesus for a sign. Like me, they had ignored the many signs taking place right in front of them. Jesus had healed the sick, cast out demons, and even raised the dead. What they were really looking for was an excuse to *not* accept the obvious. Jesus responded to them by referring to the weather. He described the clear meaning of a red sky at night and then told them, "You know how to interpret the appearance of the sky, but you cannot interpret the signs of the times" (Mt. 16:3). Yes, I already had all the signs I needed that morning. Red sky at night meant no concert tonight. I simply didn't want to believe it. The religious leaders already had their sign as well. Oh, if they only knew what awaited them if they simply believed.

## Waterlines

# 41. Dangling Feet

*If your hand or your foot causes you to sin*
*cut it off and throw it away.*
*(Mt. 18:8)*

## River Cruise
*Read Matthew 18:1–14*

## River Reflections

My family spent our vacations at Elim Lodge for the fellowship and, almost as importantly, for the Muskies. The Kawartha Lakes in Ontario, Canada are well known for their Muskellunges. Every day we would all go out and do our best to catch a Muskie. Then, every evening the men would sit around and tell their fish stories (as I sat in the corner listening with fascination). How many were just fish tales, I'll never know for sure but one story, in particular, I will never forget. A young boy had been sitting at the end of the dock dangling his feet in the water. Apparently the wiggling toes appeared to the giant three foot Muskie lurking below the dock as the perfect snack. It lurched out of the water and grabbed the boy's entire foot with its razor-sharp teeth. As the story goes, the boy ultimately got the fish but he lost a toe. Whether it really happened this way or not, I would not advocate this as a method of Muskie fishing.

In cautioning His disciples on the importance of protecting themselves from the temptation of sin Jesus used the illustration of cutting off one's foot. He added, "It is better for you to enter life maimed or crippled than to have two hands or two feet and be thrown into eternal fire" (Mt. 18:8). Jesus was obviously not advocating this as a method of keeping oneself pure. That was already taken care of at the Cross. His point was that if something is likely to entrap you, avoid it at all costs. Don't dangle your toes in dangerous waters and risk falling victim to Satan's razor-sharp teeth. The brief pleasure you might gain will, in the long run, cost you a lot more than a toe.

## *Waterlines*

# 42. The Days of Noah

*As it was in the days of Noah, so it will be at the coming of the Son of Man.*
*(Mt. 24:37)*

## River Cruise
*Read Matthew 24:32–42*

## River Reflections
It certainly didn't meet U.S. Coast Guard specifications. There were no personal flotation devices, flares, or even an anchor. And as far as a lifeboat? Actually, this giant floating vessel *was* the lifeboat and its passengers the only survivors in the largest water disaster in history. What's most amazing is that rain hadn't even been in the forecast. Or, had it? Perhaps people just weren't listening. Noah was building an ark. He couldn't have hidden a 450-foot wooden boat that took years to build, even if he had wanted to. But Noah was simply obeying God who had told him there was going to be a flood. You can't get a more reliable weather forecast than that. So Noah committed himself to the task of building a giant, sea-worthy vessel. It may not have met Coast Guard standards but it met God's. And when the floods came, the ark carried Noah, his family, and pairs of every animal on earth safely

through the storm. Those who laughed at Noah before were no longer laughing. In fact they simply no longer were.

We look back at the people living in the days of Noah and wonder how they could have been so ignorant. Noah clearly had the inside scoop of the coming disaster and was obediently preparing for it. When it came, he was ready. No one else was. But before we are too hard on them, remember, Jesus used the example of Noah to describe how things will be when he returns. Those who know and love the Lord will be ready for his return. The rest will not. When he comes, those who are prepared will be spared from the coming storm. He will carry his own away in his lifeboat to spend eternity with him. Will you be onboard?

## Waterlines

# 43 Hooked On Fishin'

*As Jesus walked beside the Sea of Galilee, he*
*saw Simon and his brother Andrew casting a net*
*into the lake, for they were fishermen.*
*"Come, follow me," Jesus said, "and I will*
*make you fishers of men."*
*(Mk. 1:16–17)*

## River Cruise
Read Mark 1:9–19

## River Reflections
It was, without a doubt, the biggest fish I ever *didn't* catch. I
was sitting on the dock fishing with my one and only choice
in lures—worms. I felt a small tug and began to reel in what
would have been about my twentieth sardine-sized perch. I
noticed the fish had managed to swallow the entire hook
which meant I would have a messy job getting it off. Just as
my fine catch reached the surface, something else did, as well.
A giant tooth-filled mouth broke the surface, swallowed the
perch in one mighty gulp and then disappeared immediately
back into the depths below. I jumped to my feet as my rod literally bent in half. In the quick glimpse I had, the monster on
my line was one of the biggest Northern Pikes I had ever

seen. I began envisioning my picture in the local paper holding my record breaking catch. However, the moment was short lived. With the hook hidden deep in the perch's belly, there was nothing to snag the giant pike. He merely shook his massive head, snapped the line and swam away with his somewhat indigestible lunch.

Now any fisherman knows the futility of trying to catch fish without a hook. Certainly, Jesus did. He told His disciples that he was going to make them fishers of men. But sending them out to convince people to believe in him using mere words and human reason would be like sending them out without hooks. Jesus gave them something much better. He promised his Holy Spirit would go before them, preparing hearts and opening spiritual eyes. After all, that's exactly what God had done in each of their lives. Now, he was giving them the chance to help others get hooked on Jesus, too.

## Waterlines

# 44. Miracles

*They were terrified and asked each other,
"Who is this? Even the wind and
the waves obey Him."
(Mk. 4:41)*

## River Cruise
*Read Mark 4:30–41*

## River Reflections

Jesus must have loved the water. After all, he made it. He also used it quite often in some of the many miracles he did. In fact, his very first miracle was to turn water into wine at a wedding. Next, he went out in a boat and told a frustrated fisherman to drop his nets into the water just one more time. When the fisherman obeyed he found his nets filled to overflowing with fish. I'm sure it was no big deal for Jesus to walk across the waters of a stormy lake to come to his struggling disciples' aid. Nor was it any more difficult for him to enable one of them to join him there on the water, at least until the disciple looked away and began to doubt. But when its Creator merely spoke the word, those raging waters immediately became still. His disciples acknowledged, "Even the wind and the waves obey him." Yes, these were all quite impressive but an even greater water-based miracle took place at the neighborhood watering hole.

A rather unpopular woman had come to the town well for water. It was midday—a time when most of the others had already come and gone. But rather than being left alone to get her water, she encountered Jesus who asked her to get him a drink. Jesus also let this woman know he was aware of who she was, and all she had done. He hadn't come to condemn her, however. He came, instead, to offer her Living Water. Once she had gotten a taste of the life-changing love of Christ, this once scorned and reclusive woman went and invited her entire city out to the well to meet Jesus. And because of her testimony, many believed. Now that's a miracle.

## Waterlines

## 45. Mates for Life

*Therefore what God has joined together,*
*let man not separate.*
*(Mk. 10:9)*

### River Cruise
*Read Mark 10:1–12*

### River Reflections
"Here they come" I shouted to Bob as I saw the small flock of Canada Geese swimming down the River. He ran for the bread. What had started as a fun way for us to get rid of some stale bread had became a daily event. When the geese arrive at our dock they immediate begin honking vigorously until they have gotten our attention and we come running with the goods. By the end of the summer, even the cute little fuzz-headed babies had learned to climb up next to us and eat from our hands while mom and pop goose look on trustingly. Canada Geese are known to maintain strong familial ties with the family unit staying together from one generation to the next. When they fly in their V-shaped formation it is in family units with an older gander (male goose) in the front. Another important part of this family structure is that unlike

many other species of birds, Canada Geese are known to mate for life.

Mating for life wasn't just God's plan for Canada Geese. He meant it to be that way for humans, as well. So what went wrong? The difference between the geese and us is that God gave geese an instinct that tells them what to do. He gave us choice. We are free to accept his perfect plan for our lives or to do it our own way. Judging from marriage statistics these days, our own way isn't working. The good news is that as long as we still have breath we can choose to come back to our loving, forgiving Father and try again, his way. He can transform our hearts and, if we let him, he can transform our marriages. With his help we, too, can mate for life.

## Waterlines

46. The Last Laugh

Photo courtesy Neil Phillips

*Blessed are you who weep now,*
*for you will laugh.*
*(Lk. 6:21)*

## River Cruise
*Read Luke 6:20–31*

## River Reflections

They were swimming side by side, he with his magnificent
green head and her in basic brown. Though mallards are
about as common as sparrows for those of us who spend
time around the water, I still never tire of seeing the mallard
ducks. Indeed, mallards are the most abundant duck in the
world with an estimated 10 million in North America alone.
They are ancestors of the common white duck which is why
they are so docile in nature. Another trait of the mallard is
that they are dabblers. Instead of diving below the surface,
they simply tip into a vertical position to enjoy the vegeta-
tion, insects and larvae in shallow water. While this awkward
position may cause us to laugh, these dabblers are quite valuable in destroying mosquito larvae. Even knowing that, the
sight is still quite amusing. Seeing an entire flock of duck tails

sticking straight up in the air gives new meaning to the expression, "bottoms up."

From our perspective, the dabbling mallards look quite silly. But without these ducks doing exactly what their Creator designed them to do, we would be itching a lot more mosquito bites. We would also be afflicted by many more of the diseases they carry. There are people who think that being a Christian is quite silly. Perhaps you've experienced their ridicule. God will eventually and abundantly make up to his people whatever they suffer in this life for his name's sake. Until then, he has sent us into the world to offer it salvation from the fatal disease of sin. Some will laugh at us and reject the message. A few will realize that we've been sent from their Creator and will gratefully accept his gift of life. Then, it will be our turn to laugh . . . with joy!

## Waterlines

# 47. Let It Shine

> *No one lights a lamp and puts it in a place*
> *where it will be hidden, or under a bowl.*
> *Instead he puts it on its stand, so that those*
> *who come in may see the light.*
> *(Lk. 11:33)*

## River Cruise
*Read Luke 11:14–36*

## River Reflections

One of the reasons that my husband and I like lighthouses so
much is because there are so many of them near our camp. In
the not-too-distant past, the St. Lawrence Seaway was completely dependent on its string of lighthouses guiding the
ships down its narrow channels. Tibbett's Point Lighthouse in
Cape Vincent stands at the mouth of Lake Ontario marking
the entrance to the seaway. Rock Island Lighthouse is just a
few miles farther at Fisherman's Landing. Alexandria Bay's
sharp turn is marked by the Sunken Rock Lighthouse. And
just across the channel from our camp stands Sisters Island
Lighthouse. We originally had no idea that Sisters Island
Lighthouse actually *was* a lighthouse. The building it was
housed in didn't look much like a lighthouse and, more
importantly, it was never lit. It was only after hearing a

history of the Thousand Island lighthouses we discovered that prior to the 1960's when the light was replaced by a channel marker Sisters was, indeed, a fully operational lighthouse.

Jesus has called each of His followers to be lights to the world. Unfortunately, like Sisters Lighthouse, many of us don't look much like lighthouses in the way we choose to live. In addition, some of us have hidden our light under a bowl by not sharing our faith with others. One of my favorite lighthouse paintings is a work entitled, "I am the Light" by the Christian artist, Danny Hahlbohm. In it, a tall lighthouse is brilliantly shining over a dark and raging sea. The rays of light coming from the lighthouse are in the form of a cross. Superimposed behind the lighthouse the nail-scarred hands of Jesus are reaching out. Jesus truly is the Light of the world and he wants us to be his shining lighthouses, too.

## Waterlines

## 48. The Edmund Fitzgerald

*But God said to him, "You fool! This very night your
life will be demanded from you. Then who will get
what you have prepared for yourself?"*
*(Lk. 12:20)*

### River Cruise
*Read Luke 12:16–31*

### River Reflections
The ocean isn't the only body of water that has taken down
ships. The angry waters of the Great Lakes have also proven
they have the power to overcome one of these mighty vessels.
The oceangoing *Titantic* was, no doubt, the most famous of
ships lost at sea due, in part, to its makers' claims that it was
the most unsinkable vessel ever made. Nevertheless, the mys-
terious fate of *Edmund Fitzgerald* on Lake Superior was a no
less dramatic story that gained worldwide recognition when
Gordon Lightfoot wrote a song about its disappearance. In
November of 1975, the 750 foot freighter got caught in a gale
on Lake Superior. Between the combination of hurricane
force winds and 20 foot waves, it went down without so
much as a distress call ever being heard. Its remains have
since been discovered by divers but no one knows to this day
exactly what ultimately sank the *Edmund Fitzgerald*.

The sinking of the *Edmund Fitzgerald* demonstrates once again that even man's greatest attempt to produce an indestructible vessel proves he is no match for the forces of nature and, hence, the one who created them. Second, the sudden disappearance of this supposedly seaworthy ship reemphasizes both the brevity and the fragility of life. No one aboard that ship had any idea when they left shore that they would not be coming home. In reality, no one has that guarantee even when we leave for work in the morning. There is only one place of true security here on this earth and that is in the hands of the One who formed and controls the raging seas. When we entrust our lives to his care, we can rest assured that even if our ship goes down, he will bring us Home safely.

## Waterlines

49. Small Packages

Illustration courtesy U.S. Fish & Wildlife Service

*A man was there by the name of Zacchaeus ... He wanted to see who Jesus was, but being a short man he could not, because of the crowd.*

(Lk. 19:2,3)

## River Cruise
*Read Luke 19:1–10*

*River Reflections*

One of the highlights of spring for me is the return of the migratory waterfowl. One morning in early April, I looked out at the lake and saw some tiny dots bobbing on the surface. These little dots seemed way too small to be any kind of duck. Even with binoculars I could still barely make out the eight little round black and white objects. My curiosity got the best of me and I headed out for a better look. At the water's edge the little birds came clearly into focus. With the help of my bird identification book I quickly identified them as buffleheads. The bufflehead is the smallest diving or sea duck in North America. The name is short for "Buffalo head" due to the bird's large headed appearance. The male is black and white with a large white patch from the eye to the back of the head while the female only has a white patch on her cheek. What makes the bufflehead unique is that unlike any other diving birds it is able to take off from water without having to run along the surface. So despite its small, chubby appearance, when the bufflehead is ready to go, it's gone.

When Jesus chose disciples, it was never based on outward appearance. He wasn't looking for sleek physiques but willing hearts. In fact, that is exactly what He saw in Zacchaeus. The Bible describes Zaccheaeus as being so short he couldn't see Jesus over the crowds. But Jesus could see him, and called him to follow Him. Like the buffleheads, when Zacchaeus was called, he didn't need a running start; He came immediately. This former tax collector turned his entire life around and followed Jesus who responded, "Today salvation has come to this house" (Lk. 19:9).

## Waterlines

_____
_____
_____
_____
_____
_____
_____
_____
_____
_____
_____
_____
_____
_____
_____
_____
_____

# 50. My Lighthouse

> *When Jesus spoke again to the people, he said,*
> *"I am the light of the world. Whoever follows*
> *me will never walk in darkness,*
> *but will have the light of life."*
> *(John 8:12)*

## River Cruise
*Read John 1:1–13*

## River Reflections
If one were to visit our home one might think we went a little
bit . . . overboard. We love lighthouses. We have a blinking
lighthouse outside our front door and another just inside the
door. We have a Thomas Kinkade Tiffany lighthouse, a clock
lighthouse, and several model lighthouses on the bookshelf.
We even have blinking lighthouses on our Christmas tree.
I will say, however, that as Christ-followers we do have an
added reason for loving lighthouses. Jesus described himself
as the Light of the World. He called his followers to be lights
to the world—beacons of hope shining so that the lost might
find their way home. Perhaps that is why so many Christian
artists have been inspired by the image of a lighthouse.
I know I was when I wrote these song lyrics:

*Drifting in darkness, hopelessly lost.*
    *At the sea's mercy, churning and tossed.*
*Knowing unless someone guides me to shore,*
    *I won't survive on my own any more.*
*Then through the darkness I spotted a light,*
    *a symbol of hope in the darkness of night.*
*Now I can follow the light that I see.*
    *The lighthouse is shining to rescue me.*
*Light in my darkness, you showed me the way.*
    *You searched and rescued when I knelt to pray.*
*You were my lighthouse when all hope was gone,*
    *you led me from darkness to unending dawn.*
*Light of the world you came down from above;*
    *entered my darkness to fill it with love.*
*Beacon of light, you were hung on a tree,*
    *now shining from Sonrise to eternity.*
*Light in my darkness, you showed me the way.*
    *You searched and rescued when I knelt to pray.*
*Once lost in darkness to helplessly roam,*
    *now led by your light I can find my way home.*

© Patty Mondore, 2000

*Waterlines*

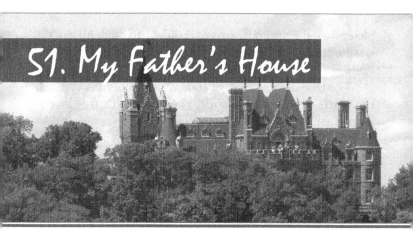

# 51. My Father's House

*In my Father's house are many rooms; if it were not so, I would have told you. I am going there to prepare a place for you.*
*(John 14:2)*

## River Cruise
*Read John 14:1–14*

## River Reflections

It was the stuff fairytales are made of . . . and Greek tragedies. No trip to the Thousand Islands is complete without experiencing Boldt Castle. Work for this six-story, 120-room replica of a Rhineland castle began in 1900 by George Boldt as a gift to his beloved wife Louise on her 42nd birthday. Boldt, son of a poor Prussian family, came to the United States as a teenager in the 1860's. Starting with nothing, he worked hard and came to be the most successful hotel manager in America. Though he became extremely rich it wasn't money that George Boldt loved; it was his wife. Louise was the love of his life. The Boldts visited the Thousand Islands in 1893 and, like so many of us, fell in love with the area. They purchased Hart Island in Alexandria Bay but Boldt renamed it Heart Island and altered it into the shape of a heart. Four years, 300 workmen, and $2.5 million dollars later the castle was nearly complete when the telegram arrived. Louise had died. All work was stopped, and George Boldt never set foot on the island again.

The true story of George and Louise Boldt has captured the hearts of people worldwide. There is another true love story treasured even more by individuals all over the world. Like the Boldts, death plays an important role in this story. Far from being tragic, however, this story promises a marvelously happy ending. Jesus died for his beloved—his Church. But he rose up from death and returned to his heavenly home to do a little construction work of his own. What now awaits every believer far exceeds the wonder of a castle on an island. He has gone ahead to prepare a place where we will dwell in eternal paradise with our Beloved.

## Waterlines

## 52. The Other Castle

*I came from the Father and entered the world; now I
am leaving the world and going back to the Father.*
(*John 16:28*)

### River Cruise
*Read John 17:13–24*

### River Reflections

Until recently, when I told people that I used to sing and play
the piano in a castle on an island they would ask if I meant
Boldt Castle. I would typically respond, "No, the *other* castle."
Singer Castle is located on Dark Island near Chippewa Bay.
The castle was built for Frederick Bourne, President of the
Singer Sewing Machine Company in 1903. It was built by
world-renowned architect, Ernest Flagg, and was based on
the castle in Sir Walter Scott's *Woodstock,* complete with dun-
geons and secret passageways. The castle was sold to the
Harold Martin Evangelistic Association in 1965. The Martins
renamed it Jorstadt Castle and opened its doors to the public
for Sunday worship services. Dr. and Mrs. Martin's dream
was to use the wonder of Jorstadt Castle as a means of sharing God's love with all who walked through its doors. They
invited me to sing and play at many of those services. After

the Martins passed away, the castle was sold to Dark Island Tours, Inc, and its name was changed to Singer Castle. Today, it is no longer the *other* castle but is as popular a tourist destination as Boldt Castle.

The Martins saw their castle (and rightly so) as a temporary home. While they lived there, they used it to point others to a more permanent residence that they have both now relocated to. The Bible tells us this life is, indeed, temporary and short. But God has opened the doors to his kingdom to the public and invited all to enter his private home. Jesus said, "In my Father's house are many mansions" and that "I am the way . . ." (John 14:1, 6). Those who choose to follow him will leave this world one day and finally get to experience the other castle.

## Waterlines

# 53. Salties and Lakers

*Then the apostles and elders, with the whole church,
decided to choose some of their own men and send
them to Antioch with Paul and Barnabas.*

*(Acts 15:22)*

## River Cruise

Read Acts 15:22–35

## River Reflections

They look gigantic from a distance but you can't really comprehend the immensity of a freighter until you come right up alongside one in a small boat. Ship chasing is a favorite pastime of many of us boaters on the River. Though I do use the word "chasing" somewhat loosely since seaway ships are required to stay within a speed limit of approximately 5–10 miles per hour. That makes them all the more tempting to check out by boat. It is a somewhat indescribable experience riding the wake of one of these enormous vessels in an aluminum outboard. The two major classifications of seaway vessels are the "Salties" that are ocean worthy, and the "Lakers" which are designed specifically and solely for the inland waterways. Lakers can range anywhere from 500 to 1,000 feet long. While some of the lakers are actually longer and wider than the *Queen Elizabeth II*, they are not ocean worthy. That takes a different kind of vessel. Salties were designed to handle the high seas.

The combination of salties and lakers, each serving their own particular and necessary function, form a network of vessels that one might compare to the structure of the Church. We, too, are made up of salties and lakers. Many of us are called to use our gifts and talents in our own local church. Those who do, operate in a similar capacity to the lakers. Others, however, are called to the mission field. Salties are those God considered to be ocean worthy and sent them abroad. They, too, are using their gifts and talents as they labor in other lands. Together, we form God's mighty fleet of vessels working together to carry the precious cargo of his love from our own backyard to "the uttermost part of the earth."

## Waterlines

# 54. Survivor

> *But now I urge you to keep up your courage,*
> *because not one of you will be lost;*
> *only the ship will be destroyed.*
> *(Acts 27:22)*

## River Cruise
*Read Acts 27:9–25*

## River Reflections
When it came down to choosing between the pilot of the ship and one of the prisoners, the guard opted for the pilot. Wouldn't you? But that decision nearly cost him his life. The Apostle Paul was, at his own request, being taken to Rome to present his case to Caesar. He and several other prisoners had been placed in the custody of a centurion whose assignment was to deliver them safely to Rome. This meant getting him there by ship. The seasoned pilot saw no reason for concern. Paul, however, was operating under a different Pilot's command. The Lord had warned Paul of the perils that awaited them if they took this trip, and he who created the winds and the seas would certainly know. Sure enough, a little way into the journey, the ship was hit by a nor'easter. The pilot quickly lost control of the ship and they were forced to drift helplessly along with the wind. They took such a violent battering

from the storm, for so many days that they finally gave up all hope of being saved.

But at that point, that same prisoner who had urged them not to go spoke again. This time they listened. Paul told the weary men that the Lord had sent an angel to assure him, "Do not be afraid, Paul. You must stand trial before Caesar; and God has graciously given you the lives of all who sail with you." Despite their lack of cooperation, God's plan for Paul would not be thwarted. Nor will his plan for you. There is no person, no act of nature, in fact, absolutely nothing that can come between you and the Lord's plan for your life if you give him the helm and let him be the Pilot of your ship.

## Waterlines

## 55. Survivor II: The Sequel

*So keep up your courage, men, for I have faith in God
that it will happen just as he told me. Nevertheless,
we must run aground on some island.*

(Acts 27:25–26)

### River Cruise
Read Acts 27:33–44

### River Reflections
The TV show, "Survivor" captured the entire nation's fascination. A group of real-life people were dropped on an island. Each week one person was eliminated from the group. The one who survived until the end was guaranteed a million dollars. Winning required living for an extended period of time under primitive conditions, eating weird food and, at the same time, keeping in the good graces of their fellow survivalists since they were the ones casting the votes. Almost 2,000 years earlier another group of people were dropped on an island but for this survival story there were no rolling cameras and no million dollar prize. As God had promised, the Apostle Paul and everyone else onboard survived the shipwreck. But from there, they ended up stranded on an island.

The castaways soon discovered they were on an island called Malta. Their first test of survival was to meet the natives who turned out to be gracious hosts. Then, there was the snake! As Paul was starting a fire, a poisonous viper latched onto his arm which, to his native onlookers, was a sure death sentence. When they realized that nothing was going to happen to him they decided Paul must be a god. So they took him to their leader's home. There, this weary survivor proved once again he was more concerned about the needs others than himself. He miraculously healed the leader's sick father followed by everyone else they brought to him after the news got out. He also introduced them to the Source of his healing power. Paul didn't just survive his experience on the island, he thrived, and he did it by helping others. He didn't win a million dollars but then no amount of money can compare to the eternal reward Paul knew awaited him.

## Waterlines

# 56. Born to Fly

> ...because through Christ Jesus the law of the Spirit
> of life set me free from the law of sin and death.
> *(Rom. 8:2)*

## River Cruise
*Read Romans 7:14–8:2*

## River Reflections
I watched the magnificent loon as it slowly made its way
down the River's main channel occasionally disappearing
below the surface as he dove for fish. Loons are excellent
divers. They are even better flyers reaching speeds of up to
100 MPH. What loons can't do very well is walk. Their legs are
set far back on their bodies, which enables them to swim and
dive with great ease but leaves them almost helpless on land.
A loon that is stranded on land will usually die since they are
unable to take off. Sometimes loons mistakenly land on shiny
surfaces such as wet pavement or small ponds and will not
survive unless someone intervenes on their behalf. This
recently happened in our area. A migrating loon had landed
in a small farm pond and was unable to take off. Someone
saw the struggling creature's dire situation and contacted a
local wildlife organization. They sent a wildlife expert who

was able to capture the loon in a net and release it into a nearby lake where it was able to take off and safely continue its journey south. This loon story had a happy ending.

The helpless loon reminded me of the situation we humans found ourselves in. Loons were designed to fly, not to walk. We were created to soar through life in perfect communion with God. When sin entered this utopian scene we were suddenly separated from him—grounded. We would have faced certain death unless someone intervened on our behalf. Someone did. Jesus came to our rescue. Those who accept his lovingly extended hand will be lifted out of our hopeless situation. We can joyfully join him in his glorious and eternal kingdom. Thanks to Jesus, the human story has a happy ending, too.

## Waterlines

# 57. Synchronous Swimming

*Rejoice with those who rejoice;*
*mourn with those who mourn.*
*(Rom. 12:15)*

## River Cruise
*Read Romans 12:3–16*

## River Reflections
Every fall we get to see the migratory birds making their
annual stopover on their way south. Over the years, we have
observed buffleheads, grebes, pintails, mergansers, the
Canada Geese and even an occasional loon spend a few days
on our small lake. I love this time of year and check every
morning to see what new visitor might have arrived
overnight. One morning, I looked out and saw nothing
swimming on the lake at all. But just as I started to turn
away I saw a movement out of the corner of my eye and
turned to discover that right where I had just been looking,
an entire flock of mergansers were swimming. "How in the
world did I miss that?" I wondered. Then, as suddenly as
they had appeared, they were gone. The whole flock had
dived, simultaneously, below the surface. In a few moments
they reappeared again in perfect synchrony. I watched in awe

as they dove and surfaced over and over moving through the water in perfect formation in one flowing motion.

What a beautiful picture the mergansers made of how Christ intended his Church here on earth to be. When one member suffers, the rest of us willingly come alongside and go through it with him. When another member is rejoicing, we can all share in his joy. However, if we allow petty differences to come between us or cause divisions among us, we destroy the perfect unity God intended us to have with each other. This unity is not just for our own mutual benefit but brings glory to our Lord as well. Even the synchronous swimming of the mergansers can't compare to the wonder of God's people when, through his Spirit within us, we join together in one flowing motion of love.

*Waterlines*

# 58. The Ripple Effect

*. . . for they drank from the spiritual rock that accompanied them, and that rock was Christ.*
*(1 Cor. 10:4)*

## River Cruise
*Read Acts 2:36–47*

## River Reflections
The wind was dead calm. The water was like glass. I sat on the end of the dock in silent, almost reverent wonder, not wanting to disturb this tranquil scene. I soon learned that others, however, apparently see still waters as an open invitation to be disturbed. A father and his young son wandered up to the water's edge. At first, they stood side by side just quietly appreciating the beauty. But the temptation was just too great. The little boy picked up the biggest rock he could find and tossed it as hard as he could into the lake immediately setting the still water into motion. Giant circular ripples rolled outward from the point where the rock had entered. Long after the rock had settled at the bottom of the lake, the ripples continued to spread out from their central starting point. The little guy clapped his hands gleefully over the commotion he had managed to create all with one single rock.

A single rock, I thought to myself, is all it took to set the entire Christian faith into motion. Jesus Christ, who the Bible refers to as the Rock, came down from Heaven setting off a ripple effect that will continue on into eternity. When he returned to Heaven, Jesus left but a handful of ordinary men to carry the message of salvation to the world. Ordinary, yes! But ill-equipped? Not in the least! When a rock falls on the ground, that's where it ends. But when a rock falls into water, it sets off a motion that nothing can stop. Baptized not just by water, but with the Holy Spirit, these ordinary men spread the message of Jesus, the Rock of their Salvation to the entire world. We are still feeling the ripple effect today.

## Waterlines

## 59. The Lifeboat

> *No temptation has overtaken you but such as is
> common to man; and God is faithful,
> who will . . . provide the way of escape also,
> that you may be able to endure it.*
> *(1 Cor. 10:13 NAS)*

### River Cruise
*Read 1 Corinthians 10:1–13*

### River Reflections
When the River finally freezes over and camp is closed for the
season I almost immediately start daydreaming about
Florida. One of our favorite places to visit is Ft. Lauderdale
because it is a city full of waterways. Because of its many
canals all along the Intercostal Waterway it has been nick-
named the "Venice of the East". There's a marina on almost
every corner and one can get almost anywhere by water taxi.
We love to wander past some of the lavish marinas that host
the boats of the rich and famous. Actually, ships would be a
better word for some of the massive privately owned yachts
docked in Ft. Lauderdale. Almost as fascinating as the yachts,
themselves, are their lifeboats. I noticed that most of these
lifeboats were larger and higher powered than the only boat
we have on the River. But beyond mere size, what people used

117

as lifeboats ranged everywhere from classic mahogany run-abouts to submarines. Why, we even saw several yachts whose lifeboat was a helicopter (or, a life-copter?).

Despite their many different shapes, sizes and modes of transportation, these vessels all had one thing in common. They would enable their owners to escape disaster if anything happened to their boats. God has provided each of us with a lifeboat as well. He has promised to always provide a way of escape in every difficult situation we encounter. But, a lifeboat is only of use to us if we put it in the water and climb in. Like any of these other lifeboats, God's provision won't do us any good unless we are willing to abandon our own sinking ship and climb aboard his lifeboat by faith. All he asks is for us to trust in him and he will carry us to safety.

## Waterlines

## 60. Bullies and Wimps

*The eye cannot say to the hand, "I don't need you!"*
*And the head cannot say to the feet,*
*"I don't need you!"*
*(1 Cor. 12:21)*

### River Cruise
Read 1 Corinthians 12:12–27

### River Reflections
As we sat on the pier, an older couple arrived carrying several bags of breadcrumbs. They walked straight to the end of the pier and began throwing pieces into the water. The peaceful scene almost immediately transformed into a wild feeding frenzy. First, the mallards appeared, hundreds of them, seemingly from out of nowhere. We watched as they gently scooped up the small morsels as they fell. Then came the air raid as an equally large number of seagulls stormed onto the scene. Like miniature kamikaze pilots they crashed down on the crumbs, and the ducks, as fast as they fell. If a duck even attempted to eat a morsel ahead of a descending gull, the aggressive gull would grab the bread right back out of the duck's mouth. The docile ducks offered no resistance and seemed to harbor no ill feelings for the intrusion.

Mallard ducks and seagulls are two of the most abundant

species of waterfowl but quantity is about all they have in common. Seagulls are aggressive while mallards are quite gentle and passive. If one were to describe them in human terms, one might be tempted to refer to them as bullies and wimps. In reality, God made mallards and gulls different. Not better or worse, just different. He made us humans different from each other, as well. Some of us are quiet and unobtrusive while others are more assertive and forceful. Both temperaments have their weaknesses but both also have their own corresponding strengths. Neither is better nor worse. Just different. Perhaps God made us this way so that we would need each other. He designed his Church to only function properly when each member is contributing his or her part. No one is more important than another, just different, and just right!

## Waterlines

# 61. Night Lights

*For now we see through a glass, darkly;*
*but then face to face.*
*(1 Cor. 13:12)*

## River Cruise
*Read 1 Corinthians 13:1–13*

## River Reflections

I didn't make it to the dock today. At least not in the daylight. It had been a long and discouraging day that made the world seem like a very dark place to live in. Several people I knew were going through some heartbreakingly difficult situations. As they poured their hearts out to me I felt helpless to ease their suffering. I was disheartened as I drove home in the dark. The dismal evening news on the radio only reinforced the darkness I felt encompassed by. When I got home I knew I needed to take the heavy burdens I was carrying to the Lord. So, despite it being dark, I headed to the water's edge. I walked down the familiar trail through the blackness of the night. But once I got to the water I found it was not dark there at all. Across the water, lights from each of the homes were brightly shining. Plus, the light of each home was brilliantly reflected as a stream of light across the surface of the

121

glasslike water. Together, those tiny individual lights and their sparkling reflections made an otherwise black night come alive with brightness.

Jesus has called each of us to be his lights to the world. The light we are to shine is not our own, but the light of his love reflected from us. One little flicker can't do much but when that flicker is reflected on water its brightness is incrementally multiplied. When several small lights shine together, the reflections they make in the water literally turn the darkness to light. When we let him shine through us, our lives are reflections of God's love to a dark and needy world. And the greater the darkness, the greater even the faintest light will be.

## Waterlines

## 62. Life Saving

Photo courtesy U.S. Coast Guard

*For he says, "In the time of my favor I heard you, and in the day of salvation I helped you." I tell you, now is the time of God's favor, now is the day of salvation.*

*(2 Cor. 6:2)*

### River Cruise
*Read 2 Corinthians 5:11–21*

### River Reflections
I admit I had ulterior motives when I signed up for a lifesaving course in college. It was either that or Phys.Ed. Class. I am an excellent swimmer so I opted for the easy way out. I ended up meeting my school requirements but I also came away from that class with a whole lot more. I learned how to save lives. The course had five main objectives: To understand the value of behaving in a professional manner; To learn how to recognize the specific characteristic behaviors of distressed swimmers including both active and passive drowning victims; To learn and perform equipment-based rescue skills and techniques; To recognize an aquatic emergency, and act promptly and appropriately; and To learn how to provide first aid and CPR. Those same objectives could be applied to the spiritual realm. As believers, we have a responsibility to be trained, equipped, and ready to help save lives.

First, we must behave in a way appropriate for representatives of Christ. Second, we must be able to recognize the spiritual needs of both active and passive drowning victims. The Scriptures tell us that apart from God all are condemned to die whether they realize it or not. Third, our equipment-based rescue requires us to put on the spiritual armor of his Holy Spirit. Fourth, we need to act promptly and appropriately to each individual's needs. Finally, we need to provide spiritual CPR which is the Lord, Himself. We read, "because of his great love for us, God, who is rich in mercy, made us alive with Christ even when we were dead in transgressions—it is by grace you have been saved" (Eph. 2:4,5). I learned a lot in my lifesaving class. I continue to learn more about lifesaving every day as I study God's Word.

## Waterlines

## 63. In Due Time

Photo courtesy U.S. Fish and Wildlife

*And let us not lose heart in doing good, for in due time we shall reap if we do not grow weary.*
*(Gal. 6:9)*

### River Cruise
Read Isaiah 40:21–31

### River Reflections
Where *was* that husband of mine, I wondered. I wandered to the back of the camp and spotted him down by the lagoon. He was shooting something with the camcorder. He waved for me to be quiet so I tiptoed down to see what he was filming so intently. There, standing motionlessly in the middle of the lagoon, was a magnificent Great Blue Heron poised to pounce at the first fish that swam into his striking range. The camera rolled for another 15 minutes or so until the film ran out and put an abrupt end to the recording session. "All this time filming and he never budged" Bob quipped. "I was hoping . . ." Before he finished the sentence, the giant bird suddenly came to life. Plunging into the water he snagged a large fish. Then, with a loud screech he lifted his massive body into the sky and flew off taking the long

awaited prize with him. I attempted to consol my very disappointed husband and assured him that still-life nature movies are nice, too.

The heron had mastered a trait that all of us could use more of. He had supreme patience. His long, motionless wait ultimately paid off and he went home victorious with the spoils. While waiting comes naturally for the heron, for some of us it often does not. Perhaps that is why there are so many Scriptures encouraging us to be patient, to persevere, and to not lose heart. When we learn to wait on the Lord standing firm in our faith we can have the full assurance he will ultimately answer our prayers and provide all our needs. He will even use the time we are waiting to deepen our faith in him. Gee, I wonder if that includes time spent filming herons.

## Waterlines

# 64. Scavengers

*He who has been stealing must steal no longer, but must work, doing something useful with his own hands, that he may have something to share with those in need.*

(Eph. 4:28)

## River Cruise

*Read Ephesians 4:22–32*

## River Reflections

My husband and I had just sat down on a bench by the water with our sodas and hotdogs from an outdoor hotdog stand. Just as Bob took his first bite we heard a loud squawk behind us. A seagull had spotted what he hoped would be a free lunch. Bob obligingly ripped off a small piece of bread and threw it to the bold little fellow. Within seconds the ground was covered with squawking seagulls all begging for hand-outs. To have fed them all with one hotdog would have taken a greater miracle than that of the biblical loaves and fishes. Once the gulls realized no further snacks were pending, they moved on to the next unsuspecting picnickers. Seagulls are known scavengers. They will eat almost anything and are commonly seen in garbage dumps in such quantities they have become hazards to low-flying aircraft. They are also known to thrive at the expense of other species of birds often destroying them by pushing them out of their nesting areas and eating their chicks.

Now for seagulls, that's acceptable behavior. They play an important role as natural predators in God's ecological system. The Bible has a much different message, however, for us people. Unlike the scavenging ways of seagulls, we are not only to provide for our own needs but to consider the needs of others as well. Ultimately, however, the Bible assures us that God, himself, will provide for those who choose to put him first in their lives. He doesn't want his children to beg. He longs to abundantly pour his blessings upon them. Anyone who looks to the Lord, rather than to others, to meet their needs will find he was just waiting for them to ask. But unlike Bob's hotdog, God's supply never runs out.

## Waterlines

# 65. Moonglade

*For you were once darkness, but now you are light in the Lord. Live as children of light.*
*(Eph. 5:8)*

## River Cruise
*Read Ephesians 5:1–10*

## River Reflections
I arrived as the last flicker of light disappeared behind the hills. I had missed the sunset but wasn't about to waste a perfectly lovely evening on the waterfront. As the darkness crept in, my mind drifted along with the lapping waters. After a while I became aware of an increasing lightness. At first, I had no idea what was happening as the eastern sky began to glow. Suddenly, a brilliant speck of light appeared on the horizon and I realized the moon was lifting itself into the night sky. The path of light created by the sparkling moonbeams seemed to set the water ablaze. I watched in awe as the nearly full moon cleared the horizon and headed up into the night sky. Although the moon appears bright to the eye, it actually produces no light at all. It is merely reflecting the light of the sun.

Jesus said, "I am the Light of the world" but he also told his followers, "You are the light of the world." So, which is it? The answer can be found in the relationship of the sun to the moon. In the same way the moon reflects the sunlight back to earth, Jesus's followers reflect his light to the rest of the world. Now the moon is always being lit by the sun. However, we can see anywhere from a full moon to no moon at all. The world will only see as much of God's light in us as we are willing to share of him. We are God's lanterns placed here on earth to reflect his light to the world. As we follow the Son-lit path before us, others will see his Light in us and will be able to join us on a moonlight walk into eternity.

*Waterlines*

# 66. The Personal Flotation Device

*Put on the full armor of God so that you can take your stand against the devil's schemes.*
*(Eph. 6:11)*

## River Cruise
*Read Ephesians 6:10–20*

## River Reflections

Perhaps it was because they knew it was *their* boat I'd be practicing on that inspired my parents to make the suggestion. It was my final year in college when they suggested that I take the United States Power Squadron's *Safe Boating Course.* Far from just a class in learning to drive a boat, we learned everything from knot tying to weather predicting. The first and most important lesson we were taught was the importance of never taking a boat out without the right equipment, some of which is actually required by law. At least one U.S. Coast Guard approved Personal Floatation Device (PFD) must be onboard for every passenger. If the boat were to sink or capsize or, if someone were to fall overboard, the PFD would keep them from drowning even if they were in the water for an extended period. The most commonly used PFD is a life-jacket though certain boat cushions are also approved as PFD's.

To be prepared at sea we must have the right equipment which includes the proper PFD. God has told us as believers that we, too, must be properly equipped for the journey. If we are going to stand up against Satan's attacks we need to be fully armored which includes, first and foremost, the right PFD. Without it, we are destined to drown in our sins. It is only by faith in Jesus that we can remain afloat. The Bible assures us that "the wages of sin is death but the gift of God is eternal life in Christ Jesus our Lord" (Rom. 6:23). The salvation we receive by faith in him is a PFD that will never let us down. It is the only guarantee we have in this life and the next so don't leave shore without it.

## Waterlines

# 67. The Compass

*Stand firm then, with the belt of truth buckled around your waist, with the breastplate of righteousness in place.*
*(Eph 6:14)*

## River Cruise
*Read Psalm 119:1–16*

## River Reflections

We began the trip, admittedly, against our better judgment. It was a gray and drizzly morning and visibility was poor, "but," I insisted, "the water is calm and I'd really like to get to church." It was a route we had taken hundreds of times before. I figured we could get there blindfolded, if necessary. That was essentially what we ended up doing. We had no sooner entered the main channel when we found ourselves completely engulfed in fog. Bob slowed the boat to a crawl as we attempted to navigate through a screen so thick we could barely make out the bow of our own boat. "Just go straight" I offered, feeling somewhat guilty. But which way was straight? Without any point of reference we had completely lost our sense of direction. Then I remembered that the island we were trying to reach was directly northeast of our camp. We uncovered the boat's compass and then, despite what we would have guessed the right direction should be, we pointed the boat northeast and moved ahead. Sure enough, about 15 minutes later we began to make out the outline of Dark Island and pulled in to the dock just in time for church.

Living in a modern culture where absolutes are becoming obsolete, and moral values outdated, the Bible remains the one sure and dependable compass the believer can rely upon. In fact, it is one of the most vital pieces of equipment God recommends for our journey. When it is difficult to tell the difference between truths and lies we are assured, "Your word is truth." God's Word is there to guide us in all truth and to keep us on a steady and sure path to righteousness. All we need to do is believe it and follow.

## Waterlines

# 68. Fuel and Fire

*"In addition to all this, take up the shield of faith,*
*with which you can extinguish all the*
*flaming arrows of the evil one."*
*(Eph. 6:16)*

## River Cruise

*Read Ephesians 5:10–20*

## River Reflections

While it may seem obvious and unnecessary to even mention, the instructor of the United States Power Squadron's *Safe Boating Course* emphasized repeatedly the importance of being sure to have enough fuel to reach one's destination (which, ultimately, is to get back home from wherever one has traveled to). Surprisingly, the U.S. Coast Guard has received countless distress calls from those who simply ran out of gas somewhere out in the middle of nowhere. In fact, we have been flagged down, ourselves, by boaters who had run out of gas and needed a tow to the nearest marina. Having enough fuel may, at times, require additional containers of gasoline onboard. Though it is not required by law at this point, the U.S. Coast Guard highly recommends that every powerboat has a fire extinguisher onboard at all times. Many a life might have been spared had this vital tool been available when fire broke out.

We, as believers, need fuel for our spiritual journey but we need never run short because our fuel comes from an inexhaustible source. When we are filled with his Spirit, he provides us with more than enough of what we will need to reach our destination. The Holy Spirit gives us the words, wisdom, and strength to handle every situation we encounter along the way. We can have as much of his presence in our lives as we are willing to give of our lives to him. Our spiritual fuel source can, however, spark the fiery darts of our enemy. One of Satan's greatest desires is to defeat God's children. But God has promised that even Satan's best shots cannot touch us when we use the fire extinguisher he has provided. The shield of our faith along with the Spirit's presence within us make us absolutely fireproof.

## Waterlines

## 66. Visual Distress Equipment

> *And pray in the Spirit on all occasions*
> *with all kinds of prayers and requests.*
> *(Eph. 6:18)*

### River Cruise
*Read Romans 8:14–28*

### River Reflections
We were in the boat and running a bit late for church (which
is not a good idea when one is the piano player). As we flew
past a boat anchored just outside the channel, we noticed
someone waving an orange flag at us. We knew from our
boating course that he wasn't just wishing us a safe trip to
church. Bob turned the boat around and we found a family
of five with a dead engine. Rather than choosing between getting his wife to church and helping this needy family, Bob
decided to drop me off at church and then go back and tow
the grateful family to the nearest marina. The orange flag
they had been waving is what the Coast Guard refers to as
Visual Distress Equipment (VDE). It is required by law. In
our state all power boats 18 feet or longer are required to
have one orange distress flag and three hand-held red flares.

I'm sure the family we encountered were glad they had followed the rules on this particular occasion.

Let's face it. At times we all could use some VDE to get the help we need. When we go through rough waters it can even seem difficult getting God's attention. So we wave our orange flag hoping he will notice us and come alongside to assist us. The good news is that as believers we have a built in VDE that never stops working. Far more effective than an orange flag, the Holy Spirit intercedes on our behalf even before we realize we are in distress. Because he is communicating directly with the Father on our behalf, we can be sure our distress calls will be immediately heard and swiftly answered. And he doesn't even have to miss church to help us.

## Waterlines

## 70. The Bell

*Pray also for me, that whenever I open my mouth, words may be given me so that I will fearlessly make known the mystery of the gospel.*
*(Eph. 6:19)*

### River Cruise

*Read Romans 1:1–16*

### River Reflections

As a college graduation gift, my aunt took me to London. On our last day, we decided to split up and check some sights out separately. I aimed straight for water. I came to a dock where a tour boat was just about to depart for the National Maritime Museum, in Greenwich. Without even asking how long the trip was, or when we would be getting back, I delightedly hopped aboard. We took a short ride down the Thames River and soon arrived at the largest maritime museum in the world. For the next several hours I went from exhibit to exhibit learning about the history of the maritime, its ships, and even some environmental information about the ocean. Far too quickly it was time to catch the last boat back to the city. But not before I purchased a wonderful souvenir of my trip. When I got back to the States I presented my parents with an authentic brass ship's bell from the maritime museum. They have had that bell hanging in every boat we have owned ever since.

Having a bell onboard is actually not just for good looks. It is another piece of equipment highly recommended by the U.S. Coast Guard. During heavy fog or at night a sounding device such as a whistle or bell is often the only way to get someone's attention. As believers, we have been told to "let the sound of his praise be heard" (Ps. 66:8) and to boldly proclaim God's love to the world. We have also been given the necessary equipment to do this. The Holy Spirit gives us the words to speak and the boldness to speak them. Then he enables the willing listener to hear, to really hear so they can follow the sounds to salvation.

## Waterlines

# 71. The Float Plan

*Pray that I may declare it fearlessly, as I should.
Tychicus . . . will tell you everything, so that you also
may know how I am and what I am doing.*
*(Eph. 6:20, 21)*

## River Cruise
*Read 2 Thessalonians 2:13–3:5*

## River Reflections
Whether one is boating on the ocean or a pond, many of the
same safe boating requirements should be followed. I admit
that when I am out in my kayak on the reservoir I am not
quite as compliant as when I am making the eight mile crossing to church on the St. Lawrence Seaway in our powerboat.
And then, there is boating on the ocean. When I was little my
family went to Florida to visit some relatives. They offered to
take my parents out in their boat for some saltwater fishing. I
remember that before leaving the dock they thoroughly
described the course they planned to follow and when they
expected to return to my aunt who carefully wrote down the
information. Since taking my boating course I now realize
that what they were doing was making a float plan. A float
plan generally includes one's departure time, itinerary, names

of all passengers onboard and estimated time of return. It should be given to someone who will be responsible to make sure the boat arrives back as planned. It is always a good idea to use a float plan (even on reservoirs) but in some cases it could make the difference between life and death.

The Apostle Paul never left home without a float plan clearly in place. He would always tell his fellow believers where he was going and what he planned, with God's help, to accomplish there. Paul knew the importance of being covered in prayer every step of the way. He knew it could make the difference between life and death, for himself physically, as well as for his audiences spiritually. And true to God's word, as the Church prayed the Spirit moved and as Paul preached countless lost souls found their way Home.

*Waterlines*

## 72. Right Of Way

*Do nothing out of selfish ambition or vain conceit, but
in humility consider others better than yourselves.*
(Phil. 2:3)

### River Cruise
*Read Philippians 2:1–11*

### River Reflections
One of the first observations I made about boating is the
total lack of yellow lines to follow. Nor are there any stop
signs or passing lanes. Just open water and lots of boats.
Whenever I saw a boat speeding our way I wondered what to
do. I have since learned there are very specific nautical rules
of the road that, if followed make safe boating easy. When
two boats are approaching each other, they should pass on
each other's port side. A power vessel must always give right
of way to a non-powered boat such as a kayak or sailboat.
Larger vessels, like ships or trawlers, have the right of way
over smaller power boats since they are unable to respond as
quickly. A freighter, for example, needs about a mile to navigate a turn and two miles to come to a stop which is an excellent reason to give them their right of way. Once one learns
the basic nautical rules of the road safe boating is easy.

God has also given his children some rules of the road for smoother sailing. The instructions are easy. We are told, simply, to "consider others better than yourselves." Okay, so maybe implementing that attitude isn't as easy as understanding it. But he hasn't asked us to do it without precedent. We are told, "Your attitude should be the same as that of Christ Jesus" (Phil. 2:4). Nor has he asked us to do it in our own strength. The Spirit of Jesus, the Supreme Servant, dwells within us enabling us to model our Master's example. And finally, he hasn't asked us to do it without reward. Jesus the Servant was ultimately glorified, and is now preparing for the arrival of his faithful children who will join him for eternity.

## Waterlines

# 73. Charting the Course

*I press on toward the goal to win the prize for which
God has called me heavenward in Christ Jesus.*
*(Phil. 3:14)*

## River Cruise
*Read Philippians 3:1–14*

## River Reflections
There were charts from one end of the living room to the
other. Every time my parents decided to explore a new part of
the River they would carefully plan a safe route using the
charts they had of the St. Lawrence Seaway. Boating anywhere
other than in the main shipping lane is not recommended for
the ill-prepared boater. The River is literally filled with hidden shoals and depths ranging from hundreds of feet to mere
inches. My parents had learned the hard way that the only
assurance of getting home with the propeller intact was to
plot a safe course using nautical charts. The National Oceanic
Atmospheric Administration (NOAA) Charts are nautical
maps which cover every inland waterway in the U.S. and are
so thorough they include depth of water, hidden shoals, and
numerous other details specific to each body of water. The
use of these charts along with a working knowledge of the

channel marker system will help ensure even an amateur boater to arrive safely at their destination.

The Apostle Paul was firmly committed to reaching his destination, as well. Assured of the rewards that awaited him there he labored diligently to accomplish all his beloved Savior had called him to do. His ultimate desire was to live in a way that brought glory to the Lord. But Paul did not attempt to enter any uncharted waters in his travels. He faithfully followed the course God specifically plotted for him with the help of the Holy Spirit who God promised, "will guide you into all truth." God has charted a specific course for every believer to follow and has given each of us his Spirit to guide us all along the way. Those who faithfully follow his leading will one day join Paul at the finish line.

## Waterlines

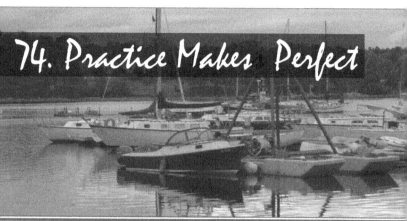

## 74. Practice Makes Perfect

*Whatever you have learned or received or heard*
*from me, or seen in me—put it into practice.*
*And the God of peace will be with you.*
*(Phil. 4:9)*

### River Cruise
*Read Philippians 3:17–4:9*

### River Reflections
I learned a lot from my Safe Boating Course and even got a
perfect score on my final exam. Thinking about it, so did my
dad. But the funny thing about both of us is that, to this day,
we still find that the best way to land a boat is to ram the
dock and hope someone is there to catch us. My husband, on
the other hand, took the helm and docked the boat on his
first try. How could he make it look so easy? We decided that,
though Bob had never driven a boat before, he had driven
everything from tractors to tow trucks and had acquired the
ability of handling whatever kind of vehicle he was in. So
when we pulled up to the dock at church with such ease it
was no surprise to me when the onlookers all commented
about what an excellent captain my husband was (and as his
first mate, I was very proud).

Another thing I learned from my class was that even acquiring a vast knowledge about boats, nautical equipment, and navigational skills will not make me an experienced boat driver. Only practice—lots of practice—can do that. The same is true in our walk with God. We can know every verse in the Bible, and eloquently win every theological debate but if we don't put our faith into action and practice what we preach, we'll keep ramming the dock. To become Christ-like doesn't happen merely by reading about him. We need to walk with him daily and allow his Spirit to work in our lives to make us more like him. Only then will others see our Heavenly Father in us and be drawn to him. And when they do, he will be very proud.

## Waterlines

# 75. Abound or Abased

*I have learned, in whatsoever state I am, therewith to be content. I know both how to be abased, and I know how to abound: every where and in all things . . . both to abound and to suffer need.*
*(Phil. 4:11, 12)*

## River Cruise
*Read Philippians 4:10–23*

## River Reflections
The water levels are high when we arrive in the spring. But by fall they will drop anywhere from one to three feet or more. Water levels are a big deal to the River community since they have a direct impact on its economy. Commercial shipping is a major industry there, so low water levels makes travel much more dangerous for some of the larger ships. Marinas also suffer when their docks end up on dry ground forcing them to close early. Tour boats can lose access to some of the area attractions. Private camp owners find their docks have become inaccessible and boaters have to deal with hidden shoals that have become dangerously close to the surface. Though the Seaway Authorities have the ability to adjust the River's flow, maintaining a stable water level is simply out of their control.

Yet, some folks have learned to make the most of the changing water levels. When the water was extremely low, a marina ended up with several of its docks on dry ground. Dangerous shoals littered the bay. But the owner cheerfully told us, "We're getting by just fine". As for the newly exposed shoals he commented, "When you can see 'em, rocks are much easier to avoid." He also added that sales on propellers were at an all-time high. Like the Apostle Paul, this man had learned how to be content even in a difficult situation. However, unlike the marina owner whose positive outlook could be attributed to his increased profits, Paul's contentment was based on a much more secure, unshakeable truth. He wrote, "I can do everything through him who gives me strength" (Phil 4:13). In high or low water, whether abounding or abased, when we are grounded on Christ we have every reason to be content.

## Waterlines

## 76. Held Together

*All things have been created by Him and for Him…and in Him all things hold together.*
*(Col.1:16, 17)*

### River Cruise
*Read Psalm 104:24–35*

### River Reflections
As I sat on the dock, an abandoned Styrofoam container floated past. I frowned, and reached out with my fishing rod to rescue this piece of discarded trash from the River. Actually, I rescued the River from the discarded trash. I have never understood how people who claim to love the great outdoors could be so thoughtless about keeping it clean. As a believer, I know that from the very beginning God has given us the responsibility of caring for His creation. He put Adam and Eve in the lovely Garden of Eden and told them "to tend and watch over it" (Gen. 1:15). I do not believe, however, that we humans have been given the power to save or destroy the earth. We are constantly being told that the earth is in serious trouble and it is all our fault. What they are really saying is that humankind is in control of this world and we, alone, have the power to save it.

It is true that our negligence and abuse of this world's natural resources have caused some devastating effects. It is also true that God has told us to care for the earth and its creatures. However, to think we have the power to control the ultimate destiny of the earth is simply not true. Only One has that kind of power. The Psalmist acknowledged God as both Creator and Sustainer of the earth stating that he "set the earth on its foundations; it can never be moved". He wrote, "When you send your Spirit, they are created, and you renew the face of the earth" and concluded this lovely creation song with "Praise the Lord" (Ps. 104:5,30). Even as I pull trash out of his water I can conclude with the Psalmist, "Praise the Lord."

## Waterlines

# 77. An Anchored Faith

Photo courtesy Janet Robbins

*... if you continue in your faith, established and firm,*
*not moved from the hope held out in the gospel.*
*(Col. 1:23)*

## River Cruise
*Read Colossians 1:9–23*

## River Reflections
My first boat was purple. I was just out of college and had
rented a cottage right at a marina. When I saw the old rowboat for sale I bought it immediately and painted it purple.
Actually, it was lavender and by the time I was finished, so
were the oars, the boat cushions and, yes, even the anchor.
Quite proud of my fine vessel I was out on the water almost
every day. The lake is actually a reservoir formed by a large
dam at one end which I was always careful to avoid. I would
row out to the middle, lay back against the bow and let the
boat drift. It was so peaceful out there I could easily be
rocked to sleep. In fact, one day I was. By the time I woke
up the boat had drifted far closer to the dam than I cared
to be. After that, when I wanted to drift I did so with the
anchor down.

There's an expression that goes, "It's not how much faith you have, but what you put your faith in that counts." I can believe with all my heart that my boat won't drift over the dam, but unless I am firmly anchored in place, my faith is ungrounded. So too, I can believe with all my heart that I am going to Heaven some day, but unless that faith is anchored on Jesus Christ it is meaningless. Jesus tells us, "I am the way and the truth and the life. No one comes to the Father except through me" (Jn. 14:6). My purple anchor assured me that I would not go over the dam. Those who are anchored on Jesus will be held securely in this life and find safe harbor in the next.

## Waterlines

# 78. Shipwrecked

> *. . . fight the good fight, holding on to faith and a good conscience. Some have rejected these and so have shipwrecked their faith.*
> *(1 Tm. 1:18, 19)*

## River Cruise
Read 1 Timothy 1:3–20

## River Reflections
The year 1905 had been a bad year for storms and nautical disasters on Lake Superior. By November, more than 70 ships had been damaged and 85 lives lost. By then, it seemed that the worst was over so many ships headed back out including the steel steamer, *Mataafa*. But the worst was yet to come. A monstrous storm sprang up from nowhere and the *Mataafa* headed for shore. She almost made it back when a gigantic wave crashed the stern into the concrete pier. The collision ripped the ship's rudder completely off leaving it with no ability to navigate. The next wave pulled the *Mataafa* back out from the breakwater where it quickly sank. Though merely yards from safely, no rescue operation could begin until the storm had passed. It wasn't until the next day that rescuers reached the *Mataafa*. Only 15 out of a crew of 24 were still alive. Those

who had survived explained that they did so by keeping active
and by dancing throughout the night to stay warm.

The Apostle Paul was all too familiar with sinking ships
having survived this very ordeal himself. Perhaps that is why
the illustration of a shipwreck came to mind when he was
describing those who have lost their faith. Perhaps he remembered how, as the weeks of being lost at sea went by, the others
onboard became discouraged and eventually completely lost
any hope of survival. Paul, however, knew better. He never
doubted God who promised he and all the others would survive. The boat eventually sank, but Paul's spirit continued to
dance. Like Paul, each of us will face stormy seas as we go
through this life but as long as we keep dancing by faith in
God's ultimate rescue we need not fear being shipwrecked.

## Waterlines

## 79. Imposters

*...while evil men and impostors will go from bad to worse, deceiving and being deceived.*
*(2 Tm. 3:13)*

### River Cruise
Read 2 Timothy 3:1–17

### River Reflections
I couldn't believe my eyes! It was Thanksgiving morning and I had gone out despite the fall chill for my own quiet time of thanksgiving by the water. There, just a little way from shore, I spotted a perfectly marked male bufflehead floating motion-lessly. I, too, stood motionlessly so as not to scare him away. Suddenly, I heard the engine of a small boat and saw a pair of hunters start to come our way. "Run, bufflehead, run!" I called out to warn my new friend. But the little bird remained still. "Perhaps he is injured" I thought as the boat quickly approached. I stood and watched helplessly. The boat pulled up right alongside the bird but instead of shooting him, one man reached over the side of the boat, scooped him up and sped away. That perfect bufflehead was nothing more than a decoy.

Buffleheads are obviously not the only creatures who can be fooled by decoys. But even beyond plastic duck models, the world is full of impostors out to fool whoever they can. Satan places decoys in our paths who claim to have the truth. He uses these people to lead us *away* from the truth to follow fakes—spiritual impostors. The Scriptures warn us, "For false Christs and false prophets will appear and perform great signs and miracles to deceive even the elect—if that were possible" (Mt. 24:24). So how do we tell the decoys from the real McCoy? The best way to spot a fake is to study the real thing. As we spend time in the Scriptures, and with the One who authored them, we will not be fooled when an impostor tries to draw us off the path of truth. Satan will have to pack up his decoys and move on.

## Waterlines

# 80. Useless?

Photo courtesy Martin Cathrae

*I appeal to you for my son Onesimus . . .*
*Formerly he was useless to you, but now he has*
*become useful both to you and to me.*
*(Phlm. 1:10, 11)*

## River Cruise
*Read Philemon 1:8–21*

## River Reflections
It was the fall migration season. When I spotted a new visitor
on our little lake, I was disappointed when I realized it was a
cormorant. While cormorants are not particularly ugly birds,
they have several bad habits that have given them a bad rap
especially among fishermen. First, cormorants are quickly
multiplying freeloaders. They move into an area often taking
over the nests of other species. They are also continuously
expanding in range and number often to the exclusion of
other birds. In addition, cormorants are notorious fish eaters.
They are excellent divers and use this ability to quickly reduce
the fish population in any area they occupy. This has become
enough of a problem that conservationists are trying to find a
way to control the cormorant population. Now I've heard that
in the Far East, they have taken an entirely different tactic.

Rather than seeing the cormorant as a problem, some clever fishermen saw potential in this skilled creature. By placing a ring on their necks, they trained the cormorants to fish *for* them.

The Bible describes a runaway slave named Onesimus who was considered by some to be completely useless. The Apostle Paul, however, saw something entirely different. He saw Onesimus through God's eyes and only saw potential. Eventually, Paul helped lead Onesimus to the Lord and watched this new believer transform from being useless to useful. By the way, the name "Onesimus" literally means, "useful." In God's hands, Onesimus truly came to live up to his name and God desires to do the same for you. Have you ever felt useless, or that you aren't living up to all you were meant to be? God sees only potential and if you place your life in his hands, he can make an Onesimus out of you.

## Waterlines

# 81. The Master Artist

*Jesus has been found worthy of greater honor than Moses, just as the builder of a house has greater honor than the house itself. For every house is built by someone, but God is the builder of everything.*
*(Heb. 3:3,4)*

### River Cruise
*Read Hebrews 3:1–14*

### River Reflections
"If you've seen one river, you've seen them all" was the reaction I got from a friend I was trying to describe the indescribable beauty of the St. Lawrence Seaway to. Obviously, I hadn't done a very good job. "Okay" I said, determined to get my point across somehow, "Do you have a favorite artist?" She happened to be a collector of Monet. "But if you've seen one Monet, you've seen them all, right?" My friend responded, "Oh, that's different. That's art, and every work of art has a unique beauty all it's own. Each painting is a different statement being made by the hands of a great artist." She continued, "Each painting is actually a reflection of the one who made it, revealing an insight into the artist, himself. You can never have too many because each one contributes to an

overall understanding of who the artist really is. The more you have, the more complete the picture."

"My point, exactly!" I said, ecstatically. Every mountain, sea, living creature *and river* is, indeed, a work of art marvelously designed by the hands of a Great Artist. Now I admit my bias towards the seaway we call, "The River." But because I've experienced the beauty of that particular river, I find myself even more interested in the other natural wonders of this world. The earth is literally covered with waterways, rivers, and oceans, each with a beauty all its own. It is because I know and love the Creator, however, that I am most enthralled with his creation for in all of it I find a reflection of him. My friend can't get enough of the works of the master artist, Monet. You might just say I can't get enough of the works of the Master Artist, Jesus.

## Waterlines

# 82. Firm and Secure

*We who have fled to take hold of the hope offered to us may be greatly encouraged. We have this hope as an anchor for the soul, firm and secure.*
*(Heb. 6:18–19)*

## River Cruise
*Read Hebrews 6:9–19*

## River Reflections

The 750-foot freighter had traveled all the way from Lebanon and was headed to the Great Lakes. But it only made it as far inland as Cape Vincent when the engine simply gave out right in the middle of the shipping lane. Cape Vincent is known for its deadly shallows and it didn't take long for the massive ship to drift out of the channel directly toward the shoal-filled waters. Fortunately the freighter had its required anchor onboard. So as soon as the vessel was out of the main channel the captain dropped anchor and the ship held firm. Now for the residents of Cape Vincent this was the best thing that had happened all summer. Tourists began to flock to the tiny town to see the stranded ship. Even the local news carried the story. The local businesses made record sales that summer. Considering the size of the average freighter, I used to wonder how any anchor could hold it against the strong River currents. Then I saw a ship's anchor. It was taller than me. With an anchor like that firmly in place it is no wonder the ship was held secure.

Every believer has been given an anchor that will hold them secure against even the strongest currents. The Bible describes that anchor as a hope offered to all of us. That hope is our salvation and it is as secure as God's own word. God has promised a glorious eternal inheritance for all who have entrusted their lives to him and, as the Scriptures assure us, it is impossible for God to lie. What a blessing to know our salvation is not dependent upon our own strength to hold on, but upon the anchor of God's word by which he holds us firm and secure.

## Waterlines

Photo courtesy Max Braun

# 83. Assembling Together

*Let us not give up meeting together, as some are in the
habit of doing, but let us encourage one another —
and all the more as you see the Day approaching.*
(Heb. 10:25)

## River Cruise
*Read Hebrews 10:15–25*

## River Reflections

The nights were getting progressively colder as we moved
into December. It was only a matter of time until the lake
froze over. The past few winters had been so mild that the
lake had remained unfrozen for most of the season. Perhaps
that is why the Canada Geese had opted not to fly south at all.
But this year was already proving to be a much more typical
Central New York winter. As the temperatures steadily
dropped each night I watched the flock of almost 1,000 geese
continue to swim around in the icy water. I wondered how
much longer they would last before giving in and heading
south. One evening the lake finally began to freeze over. As
the ice inched its way toward them the geese were bunched
together in an ever-diminishing spot of open water. When
the temperature dropped below zero that night I was sure
their water hole would be gone by morning.

The next day, despite the frigid temperatures, the geese were still swimming in open water. All those closely huddled bodies stirring up the water throughout the bitter night had prevented it from freezing over. Together, the geese had accomplished what one could not. God intended His Church to operate in a similar way. The evil forces of this world press in on us like freezing waters. On our own we would easily be overcome by them. But God never expected us to stand up to them on our own. He knew that when his people come together and support each other through the freezing nights, his Church will stand strong and firm. In fact, he has promised that when even two or three of his children gather together they will be kept warm by his presence there in their midst.

## Waterlines

## 84. The Predator

Photo courtesy U.S. Fish and Wildlife

*Your enemy the devil prowls around like a roaring*
*lion looking for someone to devour.*
*(1 Pet. 5:8)*

### River Cruise
*Read 1 Peter 5:1–11*

### River Reflections
When our parents sent the five of us kids out in a rowboat to
fish, they probably thought they'd get a little peace and quiet.
I had mastered the art of baiting the hook, and could even
take a fish off the line. That is, unless the fish happened to
have swallowed the hook. Eventually, all five of us had fish
stuck on our lines and we needed to row back to shore so our
parents could take them all off for us. We pulled up anchor
and headed home. But the sight of five perch being dragged
behind the boat caught more than just our parents' eyes. A
giant head suddenly lurched out of the water and the giant
Muskie snagged one of the perch. The rod bent nearly double
as the three-foot monster dove for the bottom. All five of us
began to scream in terror and excitement. Then, as suddenly
as it began, it was over. The Muskie reappeared momentarily

and with one snap of his massive jaw the line broke and he disappeared, perch, line and all.

The Muskellunge is a fierce predator among fish. It hunts by waiting motionlessly until a fish swims by. Then it strikes, impaling its prey on its large, razor-like teeth. The Bible describes Satan as a dangerous predator always seeking someone he can devour. Now the perch is clearly no match for a hungry Muskie. But a Muskellunge is equally as helpless against a well-equipped fisherman. Jesus called each of us to be "fishers of men." He then equipped us with his Holy Spirit through whom we can touch the lives of others as we stand strong against our enemy. Yes, we do have a predator but he is powerless against us when we are properly equipped.

## Waterlines

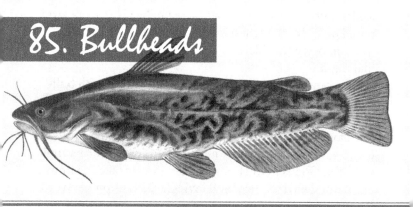

## 85. Bullheads

*Through these he has given us his very great and precious promises, so that through them you may participate in the divine nature and escape the corruption in the world caused by evil desires.*
*(2 Pet. 1:4)*

### River Cruise
*Read 2 Peter 1:1–11*

### River Reflections
"Why do you have to be so bullheaded?" I heard the woman tell her husband in frustration as they walked past me. I chucked to myself as I pictured a whiskery-faced fish. The bullhead is also known as a catfish or, appropriately, a horned pout. It is a scale-less fish with eight chin whiskers around its mouth. The bullhead feeds on nearly everything it finds thus earning its reputation as a bottom feeder. Bullheads also have sharp spines with glands at their base that secrete a mild but painful venom when threatened. I would know. I was stung once while trying to take one off the hook. After that, I had nothing but disdain for the ugly creatures. When the waitress at a fancy restaurant informed us that the special of the day was bullhead I laughed at the thought of a gourmet bottom

feeder. But she assured us that these bullheads were all farm-raised on only the highest quality foods, had a lovely sweet taste and were considered a delicacy. I still ordered chicken that night.

In some ways, we do share a few similarities with bullheads. All of us are sinners by nature. You might as well call us bottom feeders looking out primarily for ourselves. We, too, have our own form of venomous spines in the words we use towards others. We are quite undesirable in our natural state. But God is in the farming business. He takes us from our natural environment and lovingly feeds us on his Word. He transforms us from being ugly creatures to participants in the divine nature. By his Spirit at work within us, he restores us to what he created us to be; the image of himself. Now that's beautiful! Maybe next time I *will* order the bullhead.

## Waterlines

## 86. Mahogany

*So I will always remind you of these things,
even though you know them and are firmly
established in the truth you now have.
(2 Pet. 1:12)*

### River Cruise
*Read 2 Peter 1:10–21*

### River Reflections

We gazed in admiration as a lovely mahogany runabout
cruised by. Though we realize we will probably never own
one, we enjoy these classic beauties enough to become mem-
bers of the Antique Boat Museum in Clayton. That is where
we took our first classic wooden speedboat ride. Obviously
our captain took the "speed" part quite literally. He spotted a
giant tanker across the channel and raced over for a closer
look. A much closer look. As we approached the ship's stern
at full throttle we spotted the ship's gigantic wake just as our
captain steered directly into it. We braced ourselves for the
impact. If our aluminum boat had hit such a massive wave at
full speed we'd have been in big trouble. But as the 1929
mahogany Hacker-Craft effortlessly plowed through the
wave, we scarcely felt a bump.

There are basically two kinds of boats: those that plane and displacement boats. Our aluminum boat was made to plane. Because it is so light it rides on top of the water. The problem is that planing puts the boat at the mercy of the water's surface conditions. On rough days we've been bounced and pounded so hard it gave me a stomach ache. Displacement boats do not ride above the water. They cut through it. Surface waves or choppy water are no problem for them. They just push it aside and plow on through. They are like those who go through life by faith and not by feelings. Those who live by their feelings will have a choppy ride as they try to plane over life's ups and downs. But those who are "firmly established in the truth" will barely feel a bump when they hit rough waters. So why ride in aluminum when you can choose mahogany?

## Waterlines

# 87. It Is Well

> *Dear friend, I pray that you may enjoy good healthvand that all may go well with you, even as your soul is getting along well.*
> *(3 John 1:2)*

## River Cruise
*Read 1 Thessalonians 5:12–24*

## River Reflections

The author must have really loved the water, I thought to myself when I first heard the beautiful hymn and sang the words, "When peace like a river attendeth my way, when sorrows like sea billows roll. Whatever my lot, thou hast taught me to say, 'It is well, it is well with my soul'"* It wasn't until many years later that I heard the real story behind the penning of these precious words. Though he was, indeed, at sea at the time, it wasn't his love of the water that inspired Mr. Spafford to write those words. He had just gone through two major traumas in his life. First, he was completely ruined financially by the great Chicago fire of October 1871. Then, just a short time later, while crossing the Atlantic, all four of his daughters died when the ship they were on, the *S.S. Ville*, collided with another ship and went down at sea. He received the tragic news by telegram from his wife who simply wrote,

"Saved, alone." Mr. Spafford boarded another ship crossing the Atlantic and asked to be notified when they passed over the spot where his daughters died. It was there he prayerfully wrote the words, "It Is Well With My Soul."

No, it wasn't his love of the sea that inspired Mr.Spafford to write the lyrics that have blessed countless others for over a century now. It was, instead, his love of the Savior. Only a deep passion for his God, and complete confidence in his goodness could have enabled him to state with such certainty in the midst of such loss, "Though Satan should buffet, though trials should come, let this blest assurance control, that Christ has regarded my helpless estate, and hath shed his own blood for my soul."*

*Horatio G. Spafford 1873

*Waterlines*

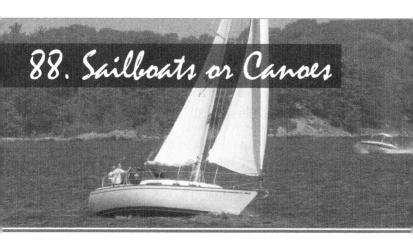

# 88. Sailboats or Canoes

*But when he asks, he must believe and not doubt,*
*because he who doubts is like a wave of the sea,*
*blown and tossed by the wind.*
*(James 1:6)*

### River Cruise
*Read James 1:1–12*

### River Reflections
The wind was perfectly still, the water was like glass, and the bay was filled with boats. Powerboats were flying by while jet boats followed closely behind jumping their wakes. Several canoes were out paddling through the quiet waters, while dozens of sailboats drifted aimlessly, their sails hanging limply above them. We took a quick break from boat watching to run into town for lunch. Less than an hour later we returned to an entirely different scene. The wind had picked up and whitecaps had begun to appear. The shoreline was now being continuously washed by rolling waves. Much of the boat traffic had subsided. The canoes had made a hasty retreat followed by the smaller powerboats. As the wind continued to pick up, eventually there were no boats out on the water but the sailboats. But those sailboats that were previously dead in the water suddenly came to life. Their limp sails

billowed out in the wind and they gracefully cut through the water. The wind enabled the sailboats to do just what they were designed to do; sail!

Sailboats and canoes help demonstrate the difference between faith and doubt. The shallow draft of the canoe gives it little stability when in rough waters. The sailboat has a keel that does down deep into the water below it making it able to withstand the turbulence on the surface. The person who lacks true faith in God will be, as the Bible describes, "blown and tossed" by life's difficulties. The believer who has truly entrusted his life to God's care will be able to ride out the turbulent times. In fact, with God at the helm even raging winds need not be feared, but instead can be safely ridden to destinations one could only dream of apart from him.

## Waterlines

# 89. Come To the Water

*He said to me: "It is done. I am the Alpha and the Omega, the Beginning and the End. To him who is thirsty I will give to drink without cost from the spring of the water of life."*
*(Rev. 21:6)*

## River Cruise
*Read Revelation 20:11–21:7*

## River Reflections
The River is, for me, the ultimate earthly place of peace, refreshment, beauty and wonder. I go to the water for rest, regeneration and to spend some uninterrupted time talking to God. In addition to all of its aesthetic qualities, one must not forget about the life-sustaining, thirst-quenching functions of water, as well. Jesus, himself, experienced thirst while he was here on earth. He also used that thirst as a way to describe our spiritual need along with his ability to meet that need. He told the woman he encountered at the well, "Everyone who drinks this water will be thirsty again, but whoever drinks the water I give him will never thirst. Indeed, the water I give him will become in him a spring of water welling up to eternal life" (John 4:13–14). Our physical needs are, indeed, met by water. Our spiritual needs, however, require the Living

Water given freely, but only by Jesus. The woman at the well willingly received the water of life Jesus offered her and was changed for eternity.

It was important enough to God for each of us to receive this invitation that he repeated it in the closing chapters of the Scriptures. There, Jesus offers his living water once again, not to just one woman at a well, but to everyone. It was for this very purpose he came to earth. He willingly suffered, died, and rose again so he could offer the gift of eternal life to all who will receive it. Those who do will find him to be their ultimate source of peace, refreshment, beauty and wonder. All of our needs will be met in him. I would know; I came to the Water and drank. So, how about you? Won't you come to the Water, today?

## Waterlines

## 90. Only One River

*Then the angel showed me the river of the
water of life, as clear as crystal,
flowing from the throne
of God and of the Lamb.
(Rev. 22:1)*

### River Cruise
*Read Revelation 22:1–10*

### River Reflections
I just *had* to have that hat! I spotted it in the store window on
our last weekend at the River for the summer. I always hated
to leave and that particular baseball cap struck me as the perfect farewell gift (to myself). I wasn't attracted to it for its
fashion statement but for its written statement. Embroidered
over a lovely picture of a loon were the words, "Only One
River." It wasn't until we returned to the River the following
summer that I could show it off. When I wore it to the first
island church service of the season, so did two others. The
very same hat! We laughed out loud at the fashion faux pas.
But what was obvious to each of us was why we were all
drawn to the message on this cap.

Though we all love our beautiful St. Lawrence Seaway, we

are also well aware that the day will come when we will have to leave this earthly delight behind. One would have to assume that everything in Heaven will be infinitely more perfect and more lovely than even the most beautiful places here on earth. We are told that the Lord will be taking all who love him to a place that has a river of its own. The Bible describes that beautiful heavenly waterway as the River of Life. It doesn't flow from the Great Lakes into the ocean, but from the throne of God pouring its crystal-clear waters throughout his kingdom. And everywhere the water flows there will be healing and life—glorious and eternal life. Knowing that the River of Life awaits us and that we'll be spending our eternity there with our Savior truly gives a whole new meaning to the words, "Only One River."

## Waterlines

CPSIA information can be obtained at www.ICGtesting.com
Printed in the USA
LVOW04s1724120914

403829LV00030B/847/P